WITHDRAWN

Irish Folk-History Plays

By Lady Gregory

First Series: The Tragedies
Grania. Kincora. Dervorgilla

Second Series: The Tragic Comedies
The Canavans. The White Cockade. The
Deliverer

Irish Folk-History Plays

By

Lady Gregory

Second Series

The Tragic–Comedies

The Canavans–The White Cockade
The Deliverer

G. P. Putnam's Sons
New York and London
The Knickerbocker Press
1912

Republished 1971
Scholarly Press, Inc., 22929 Industrial Drive East
St. Clair Shores, Michigan 48080

Library of Congress Catalog Card Number 70-145063
Standard Book Number 403-01006-3

TO DEAR JOHN QUINN BEST FRIEND
BEST HELPER THESE HALF-SCORE
YEARS ON THIS SIDE OF THE SEA

NEW YORK FEBRUARY 1912

CONTENTS

v

THE CANAVANS

PERSONS

Peter Canavan	.	.	.	A MILLER
Antony Canavan	.	.	.	HIS BROTHER
Captain Headley	.	.	.	HIS COUSIN
Widow Greely				
Widow Deeny				

Time—Reign of Queen Elizabeth.

Act I

Scene: Interior of a mill room at Scartana, in Munster. Rough table and chairs. Sacks in corner. Cake, glasses, and wine on table.

Widow Greely: (*Who is carrying a basket of clean linen, knocking at door as she enters.*) Are you within, Miller Canavan?

Widow Deeny: He cannot be far off, and he after bidding us to come see him.

Widow Greely: It cannot be only his shirts he is wanting, and Sunday three days from us yet. But it was as good bring them, and they starched and ready to put on. (*Puts down basket.*)

Widow Deeny: Cake and wine on the table, and it is not a feast day at all. It is not as starchers and ironers he is wanting our company to-day.

Widow Greely: A very kind man indeed, and a good employer of labour.

Widow Deeny: He is kind, so long as it will

3

do no harm to himself to be kind. But there is no doubt at all about it, he is a very timorous man.

Widow Greely: That is the nature of the Canavans, since the great-grandfather killed a witch-hare.

Widow Deeny: The heart of the hare went into them. What call had he to go eating it, and it after squealing in the pot? All he did was to cut the head off it, and throw it out of the door.

Widow Greely: It is harebrained the miller's brother was, leaving home for the army as he did.

Widow Deeny: There did a wise woman prophesy, Peter would be hare-hearted always, but Antony would get the big name and the branch for bravery, before ever he would come to his death.

Widow Greely: No wonder a wealthy man like the miller to be hare-hearted and the country tossed the way it is. The Queen's troops and Lord Essex havocking the whole of Munster.

Widow Deeny: The Lord be with our own men that are hiding in the woods! It is for them I would have more respect than for any Canavan at all.

Canavan: (*Coming from inner door.*) Welcome, Widow Greely, welcome, Widow Deeny. It is very neighbourly of you coming when I sent asking you; but you are always neighbourly and kind.

Widow Greely: Why would n't we come? And here is the wash I brought with me. I tell you the Captain at the Castle does not get his shirts made up like that.

Canavan: The youngster Lord Essex left in charge? I believe he is a kinsman of my own.

Widow Deeny: I heard them saying that. He Englished his name to Headley it seems, he being a genteel young man. Canavan, one head, Headley. They say he has shirts and laces for every day of the year.

Canavan: (*Sitting down and motioning them to do the same.*) Well, it is the reason of me sending for you, I am wishful to ask for your advice.

Widow Greely: Do so, and it is likely we will give it in a way that will be pleasing to yourself.

Canavan: Now, when there is a course of action put before any man, there is but the one question to put and the one to answer; and that question is: Is it safe?

Widow Greely: You were always wary, and why would n't you be wary?

Canavan: Now, when Lord Essex came besieging the Castle above, where did he get his oats and his straw and his flour from but from myself? I treated him well, and he treated me middling well. I made no complaint about payment—I was chary of doing that—it was best let the townland think it was taken from me by force. Well, it was not forgotten to me, and what has come but a letter from the Lord Deputy making me an offer.

Widow Greely: If it is a good one I would recommend you take it.

Canavan: It is what he tenders me in this letter, in return for my services and believing me to be loyal to the Queen, to make me Mayor of Scartana.

Widow Deeny: No less than Mayor!

Canavan: Now all I want is to be safe; to keep my life, my quietness, my commodity. It is with the strongest I must take service to do that. I have but one head only, and what I have to do is not to lose it. If now, I take office, will the Queen's Government be protecting me to the end of my lifetime?

Widow Greely: You may be sure they will, so long as you are of use to them, and that they have the upper hand.

Widow Deeny: There would be safety in one thing anyway, that you having taken the oath to the Queen, no one would expect you to put yourself out at any time, striking a blow for Ireland.

Canavan: Now, as to taking the oath, I don't say but it might go against me in the eyes of the neighbours. I am the loathest man in Munster to give offence to any one. But who, unless a fool, would go hop against a hill? There is many a little thing a man will do for the sake of safety, that he would not do at any common time. To turn his vest and he led away by enchantment in a field, or to cross himself passing by a church-yard in the night time; to do these things or to take the oath, what are they but a little token of respect to something that might be a danger. There can be no harm at all in that.

Widow Deeny: The Queen might be a danger with her troops in the Castle above. That is true enough.

Canavan: Caution is no load upon any one. And it might be safer for the district to have me as Mayor than a *real* Queen's man. I always said I would like to do something for Ireland when the right time, and the safe time, would come. But it did n't come yet. I see danger around on every side.

Widow Greely: I suppose so. If every one would look as far before them as they do be-hind, they would see plenty.

Widow Deeny: O'Connor is gaining the day in some parts, the same as O'Neill in the North.

Canavan: That is what I have in my mind. Our own people to get the upper hand, would they think bad of me taking office under the

Queen? The mill is a lonesome place—the roof
of it is but thatch—any attack at all to be made
on it would be a great danger.

Widow Deeny: I wonder now you would not
bring in some person to be conversing with you
and heartening you in the long evenings.

Canavan: I am best without any person. I
was well pleased when Antony, my brother, left
the house. Some notion he would never die he
had, made him go playing and fooling, playing
and fooling, tricking with danger like a ball.
Came dressed in straw with the wrenboys one
Stephen's night he did, set my knees shaking
through his knowledge and his mockeries, I
taking him to be no *right* man. It was on the
head of that, I drove him out of the door.

Widow Deeny: He brought down his name
with his own comrades, the time he went taking
the pay of the Queen.

Canavan: It was maybe best. He to be
sworn to the Queen, I myself to be thought a
trusty man in Scartana; that is the way for a
family to keep itself safe on *every* side.

Widow Deeny: Is it alive at all he is, since he
went abroad to England? I believe there was
no word of him this time past.

Canavan: I would not like to be putting myself forward, sending asking news of him. Any
harm to have happened him, it is likely I would

be sent word. If I got at any time certain news of his death, I would not begrudge laying out a fair share in Masses for the benefit and the safety of his soul.

(*Enter Antony disguised as a pedlar.*)

Antony: Who wants ruffs for the neck, hoods for the hair, all the fashions that are in any Court at all!

Canavan: (*Getting up.*) Who is that? A pedlar. I have no good opinion of pedlars. There was a pedlar did a murder one time in Cashel. To carry away the limbs he did one by one in his pack.

Antony: I have better than that in my pack! Buying from the old, working out the new. Ruffs for the neck, hoods for the hair, wearables and jewellry, combs and laces fit for the Queen of England!

Widow Greely: Are they now? (*He opens pack and takes out a ruff.*) I never saw so sizable a frill as that one, or so much like a turkey-cock's neck.

Antony: That is the right size, ma'am. That is the way the Queen herself wears them.

Widow Deeny: What way would she get her neck into that? Sure it is like a nut on a platter her head would be!

Antony: Not at all, ma'am. It would become yourself well if you but knew how to wear it. Look here now—there is a likeness of her in

the pack (*Takes one out and holds it up*). This
is the way she is—a hood on her head—two
bunches of hair at the sides of her face — the
ruff around it like spokes around the hub of a
wheel (*Puts picture on wall*). Look at that now
for a ruff! It is quite easy if you know what
way to wear it.

Widow Deeny: Isn't that great now. And
it is like that she is? Sure they say she has her
hair dyed red like your own, since she came to
the turn of her age.

Widow Greely: Is that herself now! The
woman that never took a husband, or fasted
from a lover.

Widow Deeny: That she may be dancing
quadrilles on a red hot floor this day twelve-
month, along with her fitting father, Henry the
Eighth!

Canavan: Get on now. We want none of
your vanities. Get on out of this!

Antony: Oh, brother Peter, is that the way
you are threatening a soldier of the big army!

Canavan: Antony! Is it Antony it is! What
is it brings you here?

Antony: You need not think of the safety
of my soul yet, with many thanks to you,
Peter.

Canavan: Are you after putting ears on yourself, and you outside the door?

Antony: I heard you say nothing but the thing I would expect you to say, and you the same as you were.

Canavan: (*To widows.*) What did he hear? What was I saying? It is as a spy from Lord Essex he is come!

Antony: It is not from Lord Essex I am come.

Canavan: He might be questioning you. Why did I open my mind at all? But I said no treasonable thing. Bear witness now I said no word at all against the Queen's Government!

Antony: I tell you I am no spy. You have leave to give me good treatment, and not harm yourself at all.

Canavan: Well, now, as to stopping here— it is best be cautious—the neighbours might mislike it—they might bring it up against me, a Queen's man to be harboured in the house.

Antony: Oh, I am a quiet poor creature, will give them no annoyance at all. I am not like a daring man would have his name rising up—first over the ditches in Friesland, spitting Spaniards like herrings on a pike—wounded in the gate at Antwerp—blowing up red hot guns with a match. If ever any one says it was I myself did those deeds, you may know he is an enemy of my own, and give no heed to him at all.

Widow Greely: Little there 'd be to boast of if

you did do them. I 'd think more of a push of a pike given for Munster, than of all your red hot guns!

Widow Deeny: After giving your strength to the enemy your weakness is not much to bring home! It 's the shell of the nut you are bringing us, and the husk of the winnowed corn.

Antony: That is right, that is right. That is the way I would like you to be talking

Widow Greely: A man to go against his own people for the sake of that lean upper crust! (*Points to picture.*)

Antony: Little at all I did of fighting, but to be sitting hatching in the camp. There is no great name on me at all!

Widow Greely: It 's a place for yourself you will hatch out. You will maybe be crier to the Mayor!

Widow Deeny: The miller has something to gain by it, but you to be a traitor and poor!

Widow Greely: The rich of the world should get pity, because there is temptation at their side.

Widow Deeny: I would not blame their kinsman at the Castle that was reared to go following the Queen.

Widow Greely: It is what I was often saying, the Canavans are not much of a race.

Widow Deeny: It is what I think, Miller

Canavan, it is best for us be going home. We
do not care much, with respects to you, for the
company has come into your house. (*They go
out.*)

Canavan: Now that those corn-crakes are
gone, tell me what is it brings you home.

Antony: Did n't you hear me telling them I
have left the Queen's army?

Canavan: What were you turned out for?

Antony: I was not turned out at all. I took
my own leave. I was afeared to stop on in the
army.

Canavan: I would n't wonder at that. The
time fighting would be going on, the army is no
good trade.

Antony: It is the way it was. It is in the
prophecy I will not die until such time as my
name is up. My name being down, I have no
fear of death, but it is for ever I might live; and
so whatever danger there is to face, I am safe
facing it.

Canavan: My grief it was not for myself that
prophecy was made!

Antony: But the time we were in Flanders,
my name was going up in spite of myself, the same
way it was going up and I a young lad, and that
I enlisted to check it. And so it was to check
it again that I deserted yesterday. I thought
it no sin bringing that pack away with me in

place of my pay. I thought to find a fortune in it, where it came by a Queen's messenger from London. But my curse be upon it, there is nothing at all but a suit of clothes and that picture, as a present for the Lord Deputy's lady!

Canavan: You made off without leave! That was a terrible dangerous thing to do! Hurry back now or they will say you are a deserter.

Antony: They will be doing no wrong saying that. It is a deserter I am.

Canavan: A deserter! What now would happen to me, it to be known you are a deserter! I will not abet you! Go back now before you will be missed! (*Tries to push him to door.*)

Antony: I will not. I tell you I am afeared. If I go fighting again my name will go up in spite of me. It is here in Scartana I will stop. A miller like yourself I will be. They know us here and they will not speak well of us. Sorting the grains I will be with you—keeping the hens from laying abroad.

Canavan: (*Rising.*) A deserter from the army! And in this house! Get out of this, get out! Oh, why did I let you pass the threshold! A deserter! The thing there is no forgiveness for! Oh, this is a day of great misfortune!

Antony: You need not be so tender over me. They have not taken me yet.

Canavan: Tender over you! Is it of you I am thinking? I am thinking of myself. What black wind brought you here? (*Sits down and rocks himself.*) A deserter to come into my house! (*Walking up and down.*) Calling the whole army down upon me! A decoy duck in a pond! A wire rod in a thunder-storm! A squealing rabbit among weasels! A gabbling turkey poult among foxes! A running partridge to bring hawks! Was there ever any man put in such danger in his own house and in his own place since ever the world was a world!

Antony: Who would I look to to befriend and to cherish me, but my only brother?

Canavan: Why should a man be put in danger if he had forty thousand brothers? I will not be cumbered with you. I tell you I am going to be put in a very high station. Mayor of Scartana I am to be made. Look now, Antony, we were always fond of one other—just leave the place now, and go back for the sake of the name—don't endanger me.

Antony: Ah, you are a great coaxer. Will you wish me to go to the Castle above and to give myself up to be hanged?

Canavan: That won't do, that won't do, I'd be disgraced along with you. They might impeach me for consanguinity. You have no call to be twisting a rope for my neck along with

your own. You must go into hiding, you must
let no person see you at all!

Antony: I will hide, so, till nightfall, in the shed.

Canavan: No, no, one of the mill lads might
get a sight of you!

Antony: Or in the loft?

Canavan: Not safe, not safe—there is not
enough of straw to cover you. I would be well
pleased the earth to open and to swallow you
up out of sight!

Antony: I would n't wish the widows to know
I deserted from the army. They would be putting
big mouths on themselves among the neighbours,
shouting me till a bonefire would be lit in my praise.
Let no person know in Scartana I did anything
worth praising at all.

(*Enter the two widows.*)

Widow Greely: We have very tempestuous
news, Miller!

Widow Deeny: Very strange news indeed, if
we had but breath to bring it out.

Widow Greely: The Queen's soldiers to be
coming to this house!

Widow Deeny: You yourself that was going
to be Mayor!

Widow Greely: Indeed I would sooner it was
any other one.

Widow Deeny: The soldiers had a very
wicked look.

Widow Greely: It is hard in these times to keep out of danger.

Widow Deeny: It is, where Miller Canavan has failed.

Canavan: What is that you are saying about danger?

Widow Greely: It is much if you escape with your life!

Widow Deeny: It is harbouring rebels they say you are.

Canavan: Be off out of this, Antony Canavan, and don't be dragging me to my death.

Antony: (*At door.*) I must run—no, the troops are spreading themselves to surround the house.

Widow Greely: Hide yourself here under the sacks—they might chance not to take notice of you. (*She points to a heap of sacks in the corner.*)

Canavan: (*Seizing Antony.*) You will not hide under the sacks—it is myself they will be taking in your place!

Widow Deeny: It is likely indeed you will suffer, and a deserter to be found on your floor!

Canavan: I can make my defence! They cannot say I am a rebel—look now at all the things I might have done against the Queen and didn't do! All I ever did was to strive to keep my head safe. Is a man, I ask you, to go to his death for that?

Widow Deeny: (*At door.*) A great troop of

them indeed—and the young Captain leading them on. Go under the sacks I tell you, Antony, we will stand to the front of them ourselves.

Canavan: (*Dragging him from them.*)   No, no, every rib of my hair is rising! I am afeared, I am afeared, in the very cockles of my heart! It is I myself will go in under the sacks. Stop you here, take my coat—let you personate me—they will not harm you at all! (*Gives him coat and cap and creeps under sacks.*)

Antony: (*Putting on coat and cap and flouring himself.*) There is no fear of my life. There is no big name on me yet. But you will die in a frenzy at the sight of them, the same as a mouse in a trap!

Canavan: Settle them over me, settle the sacks over me! If they rose off me the height of my finger I 'd get the shivers.

> (*Widows cover him up. Antony sits at desk and takes up a paper.*)

Antony: Faith I 'll make a handsome miller, I 'll be picking fun out of the Captain. Four pecks one bushel, eight bushels one quarter, four bushels one coombe, thirty-six bushels one chaldron—five quarters one load.

> (*Headley appears at door and speaks to men outside.*)

Headley: Stop there, Corporal, with your men. Watch all the doors. Let no one escape from the house—(*to Antony*) I am Captain Headley, on the Queen's business.

· *Antony:* Welcome, welcome Captain. It is too great an honour you are doing me, and I but a poor trader, striving to knock out a living at the mill. I'm thinking the middle of the day is rising. We will have white meal from the wheat this year, for there's nothing so natural as the sun.

Headley: A soldier has deserted from Lord Essex's troop. He has stolen Government property. He is said to be a relation of your own.

Antony: Ah, the mean villainous abominable rascal! To go bring disgrace upon my name!

Headley: Has he come to this house?

Antony: That I may never sin if any person came in at this door to-day, but myself and the two widows with the wash.

Headley: We have information that the print of his boots was found in the soft path above. (*Reads.*) "One with two close runs of nails in the sole; one without a toe; one with a bit of another boot on it——"

Antony: The brazened backbiters! Sure that is the print of my own boots about the place! Look now, am I telling any lie? (*Holds up boot.*)

Headley: We must search the house.

Antony: We will, we will, and welcome. It is I myself will go searching before you, the way you

will not destroy your fine tasty suit. It is likely
your honour may have heard I am to be made
Mayor of Scartana?

Headley: Even so, you might harbour a rebel
of your own blood.

Antony: Is it of Canavan the miller you are
saying that? Would you say, neighbours, is Peter
Canavan a man to put himself in danger, to save
the life of any person on earth?

Widow Greely: He would sooner let the whole
of the tribes of Munster go to their death.

Headley: I believe if it were not for dread
of our army you would all be rebels against our
bright goddess, Elizabeth, the fairest princess be-
neath the skies.

Antony: Guide your eyes sideways. Look
what is forenenst you on the wall—a picture of
the Queen's majesty. Who would say now this
is not a loyal place?

Headley: Is that the Queen?

Antony: Herself indeed. (*Takes off cap.*)
God bless the man that brought it here! Here
now, Captain, is wine of Spain, you will not refuse to drink to her health.

Headley: I will never refuse to drink to that
glorious one. (*Drinks and falls on one knee.*)
But what audacious man has tried to set down
her portrait!

"All were it Zeuxis or Praxiteles

His skilful hand would fail and greatly faint
Picturing her dainty beauty, Sacred Saint——"
Queen of Love! Paragon of Beauty! Prince of
Peace! Crown of Lilies! Image of the Heavens!
Mirror of Divine Majesty! Mirror of Grace!
—oh, let me look nearer (*Gets up*). I suppose it
is not a very exact portrait?

Antony: It is maybe a little too fleshy in the
jaw—but she was much like that the last time I
saw her.

Headley: (*Drinking.*) You saw the Queen?

Antony: I was mostly reared around this
place, but I went one time to London—with samples of flour I went—they made use of some of
it in the Court. But sure you must often have
seen her yourself?

Headley: Not exactly—I have not yet been in
the royal presence. Of course I shall be when-
ever I go to England—but I did n't go there yet.

Antony: Not in England! I thought by you
that you had never been reared in Ireland at
all.

Headley: What matter, it is all the one thing.
I have English connections—I had always an
English heart. Now I will call in the Corporal
to search.

Antony: (*Stopping him.*) Look here now,
Captain, I am your well-wisher and I have a
thing to put in your mind. Go over to the

Court—make no delay—it will be a sure road to fortune.

Headley:　That has been said to me before.

Antony:　I hope it is not a liberty, saying you are a high-up lovely young man.

Headley:　I am told there are some have called me the Apollo of the army.

Antony:　I heard that—a very civil countenance—grand beautiful features—and believe me if I heard it, the Queen has not been without hearing it, for she has a great respect for comeliness.

Headley:　More than that again, I have been told that my name has come to the royal ear.

Antony:　If she could but see you now; or maybe you poetise.　They speak nothing at the Court but poetry.

Headley:　A sonnet maybe an odd time

Antony:　That is good.　Write me out one now and I 'll mix it in my flour.　I 'll take care she will get it in a cake of bread.

Headley:　I have not to go to those shifts.　I have samples of my verse given to some who will lay it in the Queen's way.

Antony:　And very good verse it is I 'll engage.

Headley:　My comrades think well of it.　(*Sings:*)

    Ye traitors all that do devise
        To plague our Paragon,

And in your hearts in treacherous wise
    Let such vain thoughts run on.
Consider what your end will be
    Before you farther go;
The Crown of Lilies joyfully
    Will hang you in a row!

(*Waving handkerchief as he sings it falls among sacks; he takes another glass of wine.*)   Essex keeps me here in this exile—there are some who say it is jealousy.   I have not the chance to show myself off before Her Grace, even to write a report.   But I go dine with him to-night to drink the Queen's health before he goes north.

Antony: Well, I won't delay you, Captain (*Leading him to the door*), I being proud to have showed you that likeness, and to be the same thing as dealer with the Court.

Headley: Oh, yes, it was all a mistake; we must look in some other place for that rascally deserter.   (*Turns back at door.*)   Ah, I have dropped my handkerchief.   (*Goes towards sacks, as Peter, who has looked out, puts down his head.*) There is some noise, a rustling——

Antony: It is but a mouse in the flour sacks.

Headley: I thought I saw something shaking.

Antony: A mouse—nothing but a mouse. I know that mouse well.

Widow Greely: (*Catching up clothes-basket and*

getting between Headley and sacks.) Your honour might want some starching done and crimping. This woman and myself are the best in the whole town.

Widow Deeny: (*Going beside her.*) Great at frills we are and anything that is for show. Lace for the cuffs or the like.

Headley: Go then to the Castle and see to my ruffles. They are not fit for me to wear at the dinner to-night. I suspect them of having been ironed with a rusty cannon-ball.

Widow Greely: We will go up there on the minute. We will follow your honour and the troops.

Headley: Very good. It's not easy to be too attentive to ruffles. (*Is going but turns again.*) But where is my laced handkerchief? (*Pushes past women.*) It must have dropped among the sacks. (*He pokes in sword. A loud shriek is heard and Canavan stands up.*)

Canavan: Spare me! Spare me! I hope I have not been thrust through with any sort of a poisoned dagger!

Headley: You are the deserter I am looking for!

Canavan: Oh, such a thing to say! I, that never left the sound of the mill-wheel!

Headley: As well as deserting, you stole this pack.

Canavan: Blessed if I ever saw it till within the last half hour!

Headley: You have disguised yourself.

Canavan: Any one would do that for safety, and a wicked troop of men at his door!

Headley: You were making your way to join the rebels.

Canavan: They would not take me if I would join them! I would make no fist at all of fighting. It would melt the marrow of O'Neill himself to hear the screams I would let out of me, and the first gun going off! They would as soon take me among them as they would weaken their drop of spirits with the shiver of the water from the mill-race! Speak up for me, Antony, and tell him who I am and what I am!

Antony: He is but a poor crazy hawker I befriend an odd time.

Canavan: I am not! I am the miller.

Antony: He has been drinking a drop too much—

Canavan: I was not. I am sober!

Antony: Light-headed he is—innocent—

Canavan: I am not innocent!

Antony: Would n't do any grain of harm—

Canavan: Let you not decry me!

Antony: As quiet as a child—

Canavan: Let you stop defaming me!

Antony: A simpleton—

Canavan: No more than yourself!

Antony: Ah, my poor Jack!

Canavan: That is not my name!

Antony: I thought you had forgotten it.

Canavan: It is you are miscalling me!

Antony: (*Tapping forehead.*)   It is easy known the moon is at the full.

Canavan: My curse upon the moon!

Antony: He is quiet at other times.

Canavan: I will not be quiet, I will tell—

Antony: Ah, tell tale, tell tale!

Canavan: I am the miller!

Antony: A fanciful fellow.

Canavan: I am Canavan the miller!

Antony: (*Sitting down on table.*)   I gave him shelter and clothed him, and now he says he is myself.

Canavan: Get out of this, you scheming juggler, you!

Antony: Go back to your sleep, my poor Jack, and I forgive you.

Headley: Make an end of this clatter!   One or other of you is a rogue.

Canavan: That 's a true word!   It is he is the rogue!   I am honest!   I am no rebel!

Headley: It was guilt that made you hide among the sacks.

Canavan: It was he hid me, it was he disguised me.   All I wanted was to keep myself safe! It is his own safety he was thinking of.

Antony: Oh, my poor wandering Jack!

Canavan: Wandering yourself! It is he is a stroller and a rambler and a deceiver and a bad character, and a mocker and a disturber and a rogue and a vagabond, and a deserter from the Queen's troops.

Antony: Look now, Captain, would you say that object to be the great miller, Canavan?

Canavan: Object yourself! I 'll indict you for scandallation! Save me, save me! I am of your own blood—the province knows you are a Canavan the same as myself—Henry Canavan, that was reared in Waterford!

Headley: (*Pushing him away.*) Presumptuous trader! Audacious clown! You must be silenced! You are both rebels, a libeller of loyalists and a deserter from the Queen! I shall have something to write a report of at last, to lay before the royal feet! (*Turns to door.*) Here, men, come and seize these prisoners! (*To Antony and Canavan.*) To the Castle now to be warded for the night! You shall both be executed at dawn!

Curtain

Act II

Scene: A room at the Castle. A bed, a chair, a window, a heap of rubbish in corner and a large basket of turf. A lighted lantern hanging from wall. Antony asleep on the bed, his pack under his head.

Canavan: (Walking up and down and wringing his hands.) Rise up, Antony, and waken! Any one would think there was a sleeping-pin in your head!

Antony: (Stretching himself.) Why are you wakening me? Is it time to rise up?

Canavan: Time! What way can you sleep at all, and go slugging through the night time? Do you remember we are mewed up as prisoners in the Castle, and locked and bolted and gaoled?

Antony: The waking is better than the dream I had. I was dreaming the people were shouting me.

Canavan: Is it nothing to you what you have brought me to, with your follies and your clowneries?

28

Antony: Brought yourself to, it seems to me, with your hiding and your crouching in the sacks.

Canavan: Would any one now think that a thing to hang a man for, to have striven to keep himself safe? Hiding is it? Why would nature teach the rabbits to hide, and the badgers to live in clefts, if there was harm in it and rebellion? And the otter to sink to the water's depths? I could have proved all that to the Captain, if you had but given me time to speak!

Antony: I spoke soft and blathered him; you would have been safe enough if you had but held your tongue.

Canavan: It was you put me in danger, making a mockery of me, and miscalling me and decrying me. He would have had respect for me if it wasn't for that.

Antony: He would not have seen you at all, if you had not gone stirring and shaking in the sacks.

Canavan: What way could I help it, and I panting and quivering the way I was? And that sword! What could any man do but call out and he getting a thrust of a sword? My chest was never in the same place since, with the start I got. Oh, tell me now, Antony, is it certain we are near our death?

Antony: The dawn is not far off. Cousin Headley said it was to be at dawn.

Canavan: (*Groaning.*) To die! To die! Is it to die I am going! (*He walks up and down mopping forehead.*) Is it I myself am alive and hearing it, that I am going to my death?

Antony: That was what the Captain said, and his men that were locking the door.

Canavan: Death! Death! That is a thing I always had a great fear of. There are many things I was always in dread of, but I think that the most thing was death. I thought I had it kept a long way off from me—I never travelled by water, through the fear drowning would smother me, or on horseback through the fear of being knocked, or any way at all, if I could by any means stop in the house.

Antony: Where is the use of raving and crying? Death is not a mill-wheel you can stop at your will.

Canavan: Death! Death! I thought I was safe from any death but maybe death on the pillow. And I had myself barricaded against that itself. There was not a day hardly that I was without mint twigs tied around the wrist, or yarrow within the stocking, or an elder leaf for protection against the falling sickness! Drinking every night carrots to clear the blood, and knapweed to ease the bones, and dandelion to strengthen the heart, and gentian to keep off fever; the nightmare charm, the toothache charm, the charm to quell a mad dog. And with everything a bit of camomile in my drink—for our grandmother lived to a hundred years with the dint of camomile!

Antony: Well, it is not yourself that will live to a hundred years. It is best for you give your mind now to what is on the other side of death.

Canavan: That is the worst! That is the worst! To be going maybe before this day is out, shivering and forlorn, into some strange giddy place—it might be with the body changing about you, and it might be getting giddy through the air—or maybe put into some strange new shape. There was a woman I heard of was put under the bridge beyond, working out her penance seven years—I would not like that, to be starved and consumed under a bridge.

Antony: Hearten yourself now, you might be put in the shape of a hare.

Canavan: I would not like to be put in the ugly shape of any beast, or to be spreading terror, rattling my chains in the night time.

Antony: Take courage. It is not likely you would be able to frighten any person at all.

Canavan: And all the rabble of the parish to be looking at me as I die! And not one I suppose will dare to coffin me, or to lay me in any grave worth while?

Antony: Never fear, if no other one does it, the crows will give you a safe burying.

Canavan: The widows might bury me in the night time; they had always a great respect for me. But tell me this, Antony, is it hanged we are to be, or is it beheaded we will be? Is n't it beheaded traitors do be? Is it not as traitors they are killing us, little as I deserve it myself?

Antony: Many a man would be proud of the honour of being beheaded.

Canavan: What way will it be with me, I wonder, and I after losing my head? And if it is in the night time the women lay my relics in the grave—is it the right head will be placed to the right body, or will I be mixed up with yourself? (*Rocking himself as he walks.*) Will I be going up to the Judgment with the sins of another man's body? Is it all your own sins I might have to answer for, and I making excuses for my own? It is little I ever did to harm any person in the world. I never drank nor beat any one. But how would I know what bad behaviour you may have had? It is likely you were breaking the law of God through every day of the year. I would n't wonder if you were drunken and quarrelsome, going after women—grasping and greedy—prone to gambling.

Antony: Cheating and stealing—

Canavan: Cursing and swearing.

Antony: Blaspheming and perjuring—

Canavan: A scoffer and mocker.

Antony: Working with witches, committing sacrilege, robbing the poor box, coining false money —what are you talking of?   A hundred-murderer!

Canavan: Oh, do you tell me so!   A murderer! A coiner!   A blasphemer!   Oh, you scum of the world!   I that have one head only, to have a body of that sort joined on to it for eternity!   I that did n't know the name hardly of that tribe of inhibited sins!   I that kept myself out of every temptation!   It is many a time I stopped in my loneliness that I might not have occasion to sin! My curse upon you, Antony Canavan, what brought you back into Ireland at all!

Antony: Quit roaring and crying, and let your last end be a credit to you.   There can no harm happen, *your* name to go up.   There is no occasion for *you* to shape yourself to be timorous, as there is for me.

Canavan: This is no time I tell you to be humbugging, and death beckoning at me the way it is!

Antony: Turn your mind from that, and give it to making your will.   Stretch out now and write it in favour of myself.   In my opinion I will not die, my name being down the way it is.

Canavan: Ah, don't be talking! How can I be thinking of wills and I so near my end? If I had a way to will my treasure, I would leave all to provide for the safety of my own soul!

Antony: I will lay out a share to do that much for you. Tell me where is it you have it hid.

Canavan: I will, I will! It is a great thing it should be a help to me at the last! The most of it is in—where now at all is it? In what corner or cleft have I it hid? I knew where it was and I coming here. But wherever it was, it is gone from my mind.

Antony: Hurry on now and remember.

Canavan: Amn't I trying to remember? But I cannot with the dint of the dread that is upon me.

Antony: (*Shaking him.*) Search your mind and think of it.

Canavan: Amn't I ransacking my mind? Have I no care for my own soul? But every time I try to make it out, I see nothing before me but a gallows and an axe.

Antony: (*With another shake.*) Summon your wits now.

Canavan: Don't be ill-using and abusing me! It is tossed and tattered my mind is. I give you my last solemn oath, my memory of the hiding place is gone. I would give the half of my treasure to anyone would tell me where it is!

Antony: Look at here now, I to find a way to get you out of this, what will you give me of your riches, to start me in some trade will keep my name down?

Canavan: All! All that I have! I swear it! I won't keep back so much as a miserable starvation farthing.

Antony: That is great. I will find a way of living will never let my name be heard but by my own customers and in my own street. There will be no fear of shouts and praises for me from this out.

Canavan: Make no delay! Save me! Oh, what way can you save me?

Antony: I will see what I can do with this. (*Takes a rope from rubbish in corner and knots another to it, twisting and tying in a piece of ribbon from his pack.*)

(*A knock at the door.*)

Canavan: There is some one knocking at the door! Oh, it is some new danger!

Widow Greely: (*Looking through grating in door.*) Are you living yet, Miller Canavan?

Canavan: I am—I think—but hardly—it is not until dawn we are to be made an end of.

Widow Deeny: We are till now settling out the Captain's shirts; he bade us make a clean job of them. We made our way up before going, to enquire after you.

Widow Greely: We were thinking it might be comfortable to you to leave your last wishes with us; there will be no one else to pay respect to them, yourself and your cracked brother being dead.

Widow Deeny: It would be a pity the money you minded so well to be going into any wrong hands

Widow Greely: The Captain ought not to be getting it, letting on not to know his own race.

Widow Deeny: Those ruffians of soldiers might seize on it, and they setting fire to the mill, to fatten that red-haired battle-cock that is preying upon us all.

Widow Greely: If you give us authority over it, we will not forget the repose of your soul.

Canavan: Be easy will you, my head is thrown to and fro! I wish I could leave it to be laid out for my soul! But to my grief and my misfortune it fails me to remember where I have it hid.

Widow Greely: To the poor you could leave alms from it to open you the gates of Heaven.

Canavan: (*Taking his head in his hands.*) Wait now—I put it supposing in the one place yesterday—and to-morrow I changed it to another. I can partly remember yesterday, but blindfold me if I can remember where it was to-morrow!

Widow Deeny: I am sure where it was twelve hours ago, the time that you were talking with ourselves, and that is under the second first board from the door.

Widow Greely: The board you drew the sack over, and you after coming into the room.

Widow Deeny: The board you put your foot upon, and the pedlar coming into the house.

Canavan: What are you saying? You knew the places I kept my money?

Widow Deeny: The time you had it in the chimney, we could know it by the soot upon your cap.

Widow Greely: The time it was hid in the stable, the bees made an attack on you through the smell.

Canavan: Oh, the spies! The peerers! The pryers! The magpies! The bloodhounds! The witches! Was ever a man in such danger and such peril of his life? To be watched and be nosed and be scented that way! To be tracked like a fox to his den! I not to be safe on my own floor, or by my own hearthstone! Is there no place, within or abroad, where a man can keep himself safe? The world never saw a greater wonder than I not being murdered for my gold!

Antony: It 's a queer thing to be wasting time talking. Bid them look for the key, if you have a mind to escape.

Canavan: Where is the use of escaping out

of this, and those ones having knowledge of the most lonesome thoughts of my heart!

Widow Deeny: Is it an answer you are giving us, Miller Canavan?

Canavan: (*To widows.*) What are you jabbering and jangling for? Can't you look? Do you see e'er a key?

Widow Greely: It is very dark in the place where we are to search out a small thing like a key.

Canavan: Search in every place I tell you. I know every place a key can be hid. It might be in the pocket of a coat—or in the finger of a glove that would be lying on a shelf—or concealed under a cloth that would be hanging from the wall.

Widow Deeny: It should be in some place. If it was a dog, it would bite you. But I can find no trace of it at all.

Canavan: There are many good places to hide it in—I often hid a key of my own —in under the ashes of the hearth or put in a loaf of bread and a slice closing up the hole!

Widow Greely: There is a fire alight on the hearth. I have myself scorched, and no key to be found.

Widow Deeny: I see no bread or anything to be eaten at all. And what is worse again, I hear horses coming into the yard. It is likely it is the Captain come home.

Widow Greely: We had best not be here when he comes. I am sorry indeed we could do nothing. But we will be coming back again to see you hanged.

Antony: Look if it might be in the key-hole.

Widow Deeny: So it is in the lock all the while. I would have found it long ago if the miller had but left bothering me. Here it is. (*Throws it through grating.*) Little good it will do you, it is too late! It is much if we make our escape. (*They go.*)

Canavan: (*Picking it up.*) Oh, open the door. Oh, I can't get it into the hole. Oh, my hand is shaking—there they are in the room (*Laughter and voices heard*), it is too late. (*The Captain's voice is heard singing rather tipsily.*)

Antony: We might make a dash through them.

Canavan: Oh, I cannot do that! I can hardly stand!

Antony: Try my plan then. I looked out there when we came in. (*Gets on chair and looks out of window and fastens rope to stanchion.*) There was a guard below, and we coming here— there is no one there now—this window is not far above a little sloping roof, we can drop on it with the help of this rope, and from that to another, and there's a buttress will help us to the ground. The night dark, the town and country to befriend.   It 's a good job the Captain has as good as no head at all.   Here, Peter, go on first.

Canavan: Is it to get out of the window we must?

Antony: That is it, and to drop on to the roof. It is no great length of a drop.

Canavan: I cannot do it, I cannot do it. I am scared of going out into the clouds alone.

Antony: Well, let me go first, and I 'll be a stay to you.

Canavan: You must not go. You might not wait for me at all.

Antony: Go through so yourself.

Canavan: I will not. How can I tell what danger there might be on the other side?

Antony: Get up on the chair and look out. It is nothing to be afraid of at all.

Canavan: (*Getting up and looking out.*) I could not face it without I was a swallow or a thrush. I am certain I would fall. My head would go spinning like a wheel!

Antony: Go on. Why would I go to these rounds to break your neck, if I was craving to break it?

Canavan: If it was a level I might face it. But there is great danger of slipping on a roof.

Antony: There is the rope to hold to.

Canavan: It might give with me. It is no

safe thing to hazard your life on the strength of a strand of a rope. (*Gets down from chair.*)

Antony: Well, hang or climb or run out at the door.   I myself will go this way. (*Gets on chair.*)

Canavan: (*Falling on knees and holding his feet.*) Oh, don't go, Antony! Do not go and leave me in this case. Oh, listen to him, listen to him singing! Oh, I am in dread, I am in dread!

Antony: (*Shaking him off and getting down.*) You miserable shaking-scraw! It 's a charm you should carry against trembling, of the right hind leg of a hare. Is there any use in striving to save you at all? Though it might be no hard job to outwit Cousin Headley. If I had but a sheet, a ghost would do the job.

(*Headley is heard singing close to the door.*)

Antony: (*Opening pack.*)   Crown of lilies! That 's it.   We 'll allure him with Queen Elizabeth.   (*Takes out dress and other things.*)

Canavan: Oh, he is coming in!

Antony: Clear the turf out of that basket— hurry.

Canavan: That basket— (*Throws out sods of turf.*) A good thought—it might cover me—the rods of it would not shiver the way the sack did. (*Sits down and pulls it over him.*) If I could get into the corner now— (*Begins crawling to corner with basket over him.*) I would be as hidden as a snail in its shell—if he does not think now of spitting me with that sword.

(*Antony meanwhile has slipped on the dress and arranged his hair with his fingers, and put on ruff and headdress. He bears a resemblance to the portrait of Queen Elizabeth. He takes up basket and rubs his face in miller's floury smock.*)

Canavan: Oh, oh, oh, is it the executioner! Oh, I feel the axe! It's as cold as amber! (*Rushes to the bed, kneels and hides his face in cloak, and remains there rocking and moaning.*)

(*Antony steps into basket spreading out skirt of dress over it as Headley is heard close to door.*)

Headley: Go to the guard room. I will have an hour's sleep before dawn. (*A trampling heard, footsteps die away. Headley sings again.*)

(*Antony raps on floor with poker. He has a pair of slippers in hand, but having failed to put them on slips them into pocket. Headley comes in singing. He suddenly catches sight of the figure in coif and silk dress.*)

Antony: Upon your knees!

Headley: Who! Who!

Antony: Elizabeth, Regina Ingilterra, Francia, Hibernia, Deo gratia, defendore Fides.

Headley: (*Sinking on his knees.*) The Queen! The excellent and glorious person of her Majesty!

Antony: You are before your sovereign.

Headley: Oh, angelic face! Where the red rose has meddled with the white.

Antony: This is the man of whose beauty I have heard—who sent me sonnets.

Headley: Oh, Queen, Queen!

Antony: I made a secret journey. I would know what Essex is doing. I turned aside. I would see the Apollo of my army.

Headley: Oh, Phœbus blushes to find himself outshone!

Antony: This is your vaunted devotion. You have been absent. You have been swilling ale. No one to guard the gates. I came in un-noticed—no one heard the beat either of horsehoofs or my royal feet.

Headley: Oh, the fourth of the Graces has read my sonnets!

Antony: That is prose. I expect a poet to talk poetry.

Headley: Oh, that I had a pen—a pen—a pen.

Antony: Go on. Essex would do better than that.

Headley: I'd say: God save the Queen—Amen, Amen—

Antony: That is getting on.

Headley: Oh, Crown of Lilies, say that you forgive!

Antony: Do as I bid you and you yet may live.

Headley: Lay orders, dearest dread, trust me again!

Antony: Then go at once and send away your men!—Look here, young Apollo, you must have the gates left clear for me to go out. There must be no blemish upon the name of Defendore Fides!

Headley: I will go! But oh, let me kiss that royal foot!

Antony: (*Hastily.*) No, no, the hem, the hem of my dress! (*Headley kisses it. She gives him a slipper.*) There is my slipper; you may carry it away for a token.

Canavan: (*Who has but just looked from under his cloak, coming forward on his knees.*) Oh, your majesty! Oh, your Grace! Give me the other slipper! Let me have it for a sign, a sign to show the hangman!

Antony: Who is this floury fellow?

Canavan: Canavan the miller, your Grace, no traitor, your Grace—put up for harbouring traitors. I am innocent—it was all a mistake— I am no rebel and no deserter—it was a brother of mine—a vagabond, a trickster, a deserter, a very dangerous man!

Antony: Let him be beheaded in my name!

Headley: It shall be done!   His head shall make a footstool for this slipper!

Antony: (*To Headley.*)   Away, go, take your men.   Go by the next wind to Whitehall.   Who knows what preferment you may find.   Wear that slipper round your neck; come to the Court wearing it.

Canavan: I will go to Whitehall!   I take the oath of loyalty!   I will take it as Mayor of Scartana.   I swear on this slipper.   (*Kisses it.*)   I swear with every grain of my power, will, wit, and cunning, to be loyal and faithful to your Grace.   God save the Queen!

Antony: Hush!   Silence!   Close your eyes! Close your ears!

Canavan: I will, I will!   I will never open them again   till such time as I will get commandment!   (*Rushes back to bed and covers up his head.*)

Antony: (*To Headley.*)   Hasten, Poet, hasten, do not tarry—go through wind and weather— think of our meeting at Whitehall!

Headley: (*Holding up slipper.*)

I flower, I flower that was a barren shoot
I have a slipper from the royal foot!

(*Rushes out.*)

Antony: (*Getting out of basket.*)   The window is

quickest. Follow me, Peter, by the window or
by the door. (*Looking at Canavan.*)   He hears
me no more than the dead! (*Gets up to window.*)
Faith it's a short life I would have before me,
my name to be as high as Queen Elizabeth's.
(*Goes out of window. Canavan still kneels at bed,
his head covered with his cloak.*)

Curtain

Act III

Scene: The Mill kitchen as before. Antony is pushing the dress, ruff, and coif up the chimney with tongs.

Antony: There goes the last of her!

Canavan: (*Coming in at door.*) What brought you running home from the Castle before me? What is it you are doing?

Antony: Hiding away things I am, that are best out of sight. Any one finds them now, will be full sure it was a witch went up the chimney.

Canavan: Well, this is a great night we went through, and a night full of wonders! The strongest! I know now who is the strongest! I am the Queen's man now. Oh, she is the strongest, a very fine woman!

Antony: What is it you are raving about?

Canavan: That Captain that has such power, an army at his command, on his knees she put him; trembling he was like oats in the breeze. If she daunted *him* that way what chance would there be for the like of us?

47

Antony: Pup, pup, pup, pup! Is it that you are thinking you saw the Queen?

Canavan: I did see her to be sure, and she gave me her own shoe.

Antony: Well, that was a great playgame! Would n't you think now it might be some one was letting on to be the Queen?

Canavan: She was not letting on. There was no letting on in it. Taller than any woman ever stood upon a floor she was! She stood up over me the same as an elephant! A great grand voice she had, pitched someway squeally like a woman's, but strong and high as if used to giving out orders.

Antony: A great beauty I suppose she was now?

Canavan: She was that. Like the picture she was. (*Points to it on wall.*) Long wisps of hair as bright as silver—eyes shining like sparks from the forge. I would sooner go creep through the keyhole than go face her or speak to her again.

Antony: Is it I that have that much beauty on me? Or is it the full moon is working in his eyes?

Canavan: (*Dragging out arm-chair.*) Set this now to the rear of the table, the same as you would see it in a judge's court. I will tack up the picture on the back of it to simulate the royal arms. (*Puts picture on back of chair, hammering in tacks. Then puts on a long cloak and a chain he has fetched from inner room.*)

Antony: Leave those vanities now for a while. You promised me a share of your riches for to start me in a new way of life.

Canavan: What way is that?

Antony: Enter in some business I must, that will bring me no great credit and will never send my name up high. Clothier, cobbler, cutler, butcher, baker, skinner, tanner, grocer, barber, milkman, butterman, was there ever a shout given out on the heights for any one of that tribe, since ever grass grew on the fields of the earth or of the sea? Give me here now what will buy out some wealthy tradesman in the town of Scartana.

Canavan: Stop your blather. I made you no promise, or if I did, I did n't rightly know what was I saying with the terrification in my mind. Would you have a man bound by the thing he says when the wits are out of him with fright?

Antony: Fright or no fright, a promise is a promise.

Canavan: And so is a will a will, and if a man makes his will in a hurry, and he in the fear of death, has he no power to cancel it and he coming back from the grave?

Antony: You said you would give me all you had, I to save you from the gallows. I did save you, and now you go back on your word.

Canavan: You take credit that you saved me! You have a great opinion of yourself indeed.

There was no one saved me but the Queen. A great woman!

Antony: Is it blind in the ears you are, the same as in the eyes? Don't you know, you crazed barley-grinder, it was I myself personated Queen Elizabeth?

Canavan: I do not know it indeed.

Antony: I tell you I did. Is it that you will misdoubt my word?

Canavan: I will misdoubt it. Did n't I hear you saying you were myself a while ago? "I am Canavan the miller," you said, "and that man in the sacks is Crazy Jack." It seems to me, Antony Canavan, that you are very full of lies!

Antony: (*Rises.*) Will you give me nothing at all?

Canavan: I will not give you so much as the point of a rush, after the insult you are after putting on the Queen.

Antony: (*Goes to door.*) I give up so. I will go join the boys that are fighting in the woods. My name to go up and my life to go down, it is you yourself have sent me out to that, and to come to my death in the fight.

Canavan: The fight? What fighting is that?

Antony: I must go join the boys that are fighting for to free Munster.

Canavan: (*Stopping Antony and shaking him.*) Is it a rebel you are telling me you are? I am under orders as Mayor to prosecute and oppress with sword and fire any rebel at all, any one that would be prejudicial to Her Sacred Majesty. Sword and fire I will bring out against rebels. Are you giving heed to that?

Antony: Is it Protestant you turned in the night-time?

Canavan: No hurry, no hurry, till I will know is the new faith the safest in *both* worlds. I'm not one to say Her Majesty to be the *real* head of the Church. But it's greatly in her favour she being such a success. And no doubt at all about it she's a very fine woman, no doubt at all about that.

Antony: Heaven help your poor head! It was the terror of the night-time set it astray!

Canavan: At that time I had not understanding. I have taken office presently. I have settled myself to the service of the Queen. I must stick to my class. What now, I wonder, are all the other Mayors doing?

Antony: Give me the price of a horse and a suit itself.

Canavan: Would you suck and consume my treasure to nourish faction? Help you, is it? No, but hinder and impeach and plague and prosecute you. Am n't I a stay and a pillar of the Government and of the law?

Antony: Ah, sure, it would be more sociable

like to be on the side of the neighbours. It's a very lonesome thing being with the law in Scartana.

Canavan: Not lonesome at all. It is happy and airy I am. Look at all the high comrades I will have, Marshals and Sheriffs and Aldermen, Sergeants at Arms, Constables, Coroners, Gaolers, Process Servers and Justices of the Peace. Grand times we will have together! Sharpening the decrees we will be! Shaping the laws to the people we will be—no, but the people to the laws. I'll give them plenty of gaol according to their crimes! Oh, there is a certain assurance of quiet and great good in settling yourself to the strongest. There is very great peace and immunity in surrendering our will to their commands.

Antony: Little good I got from commands, and I marching.

Canavan: There is good in them, if there is no other good but that they are commands. Would you be buzzing about at your own will the same as a heap of flies? I tell you thousands have been damned through no other thing than following their own will and fancy.

Antony: It is not long that the fear of the law would keep me from giving you a clout in the jaw, but that I think you an unfortunate creature that has madness put upon you by God.

Canavan: (*Taking up chair.*) Ah, you savage

rebel, you! You ragtail renegade! You stam-
mering stroller, you! You pot-picker! You hangman's apron! You scabby clown! Would you
strive and wrestle with your superior? Would you
disparage the person of the law-giver? Would
you deface the image of the Queen? I'll put
the hue and cry after you! I'll hack and
wrack and harry you! I'll give you up to stocks
and rods, and the bitterness of martial law!

Antony: Well, now, the losing of your wits
has put great spirit in you!

Canavan: Get out, out of that!

Antony: (*At door.*) Well, the Lord leave
me the three faculties, wit, memory, and understanding! (*Goes out, but looks in again.*) Here
are the widows now coming, thinking to see you
hanged.

Canavan: I'll send you to the halter and the
bough! The widows—it's well I have my clothes
of credit put on, or they'd think nothing of me
at all. (*Sits down in arm-chair and arranges
himself.*)

Widow Greely: (*Coming in.*) On our way to the
Castle to see the hanging we were, and Antony
is after telling us there is no hanging at all. I
wish I had got word sooner and I would not have
put on my Sunday cloak.

Widow Deeny: I'm as disconcerted as to go to
a wedding, and the bridegroom to have failed

at the last. We that would have buried you and welcome, to go home without following you to the grave!

Widow Greely: A great deception indeed. They say there is nothing so good for the soul as to see any person die hard.

Canavan: Well, you will not profit your soul seeing me hanged, now or at any other time. I have a strong back in the Queen from this out. I have a sure token of that.

Widow Deeny: Is it a ring or such like? They say Lord Essex has the Queen's ring, and that it will keep him safe for ever.

Canavan: What's in a ring? I daresay the Queen gives out a score of rings in the year. I have something from her own hand that is a surer pledge than the ring of day! Look here now at that! (*Holds up shoe.*)

Widow Deeny: A shoe! Nothing but a little red shoe!

Widow Greely: You are not saying, I suppose, that this is the Queen's shoe?

Canavan: It is often you have said a thing that is farther from the truth than that.

Widow Deeny: Mind now what I am saying to you. Don't meddle with the Queen at all. Sure every man she ever had to deal with was sent to the block the next day.

Widow Greely: They say there are chains

rattling upon her that no one in this world can see.

Canavan: What do you know about kings and queens? Did you ever see one or ever speak with one?

Widow Greely: You are growing light-minded, Peter Canavan, to think that you spoke with one yourself.

Canavan: Don't be calling me Peter! It's Your Worship I am to-day!

Widow Deeny: Is it Mayor you are now? It made you very consequential, you to have taken the oath!

Canavan: I'll have no traffic at all with traitors! I have the sacred commission to bring the country to loyal simplicity. Give me here the ledger. It's on that I will administer the oath.

Widow Greely: Didn't you get very stiff with taking office? Or may be it is humbugging you are?

Canavan: You will see I am not humbugging. When I didn't spare my own brother, I will not spare yourselves or any rebel at all.

Widow Greely: Was it some wind from the north made you turn about in a blast?

Canavan: Here now, don't be wilful, you yourselves will give an example to the whole district. You will swear on this book, the way I did on the shoe, with all your wit, will, and cunning, to support the authority of the Queen.

Widow Greely: (*Turning her back to him.*) The hearing is failing on me this while back by cause of cold I got through beetling the clothes.

Widow Deeny: (*Turning her back.*) An oath is no thing to be taking, when you are likely not to keep it in the end. The beneficial of baptism you'd lose breaking it, and maybe you would never see God. (*They edge towards door.*)

Canavan: (*Getting between them and door.*) Let you be humble now, and limber in your heart, and you'll find me to be kind. Sure it is through kindness I am wishful to bring you, the same as myself, under the strength of the Queen.

Widow Greely: Her strength might not be as lasting as you think. Sure the Pope has his blessing promised to the generation that will bring her low.

Canavan: Ah, Job himself that got the heavens on the head of his patience, would grow surly having dealings with ye. The world would hear him yelling, and he to be arguing with a hag.

Widow Deeny: I wonder at you to be speaking such uncomely words! Our own old fathers were in this place before ever there was a Canavan in Scartana!

Canavan: Is that the way you are fleering

at one in authority? Don't be turning me to be your enemy! Force you to take out a license for your clear starching I will! Using foreign importations you are, and paying no taxes to the Queen!

Widow Greely: We are no clutch of pullets to be frighted by a cloud or a kite!

Canavan: I'll frame and fashion your manners for you! The next day you'll be late with the washing, I'll indict you for default of appearance! Tag and rag from the riverside to be correcting the Mayor on the bench!

Widow Greely: I'd sooner be boiled, burned, baked, and roasted in that oven, and a hundred heating it, than give in to your orders at all!

Canavan: Quit now being so stubborn and so disorderly! If you are deaf you are not dumb. You'd break the heart of any man, or any two men, in the house.

Widow Deeny: It is easy seen by your talk you were never of the blooded gentry! What right at all has the like of you to bereave us of our religion and our laws?

Canavan: Is it your strength you would try against me? It is little I pay heed to your threats! The time God made wicked cows, he gave them short horns.

Widow Deeny: We are well able to revenge

ourselves.   Whatever may be done in this district,
it's the telling of the story is with us!

Widow Greely: Have we no curses do you
think?   Let there be no path and no prosperity
before you, from now to the womb of judgment!

Widow Deeny: A gapped shaving to you! And
a Monday hair-cutting! And the blood of your
body to be in the bosom of your shirt!

Canavan: I'll not let you quit this till I'll get
you hunted with hounds!   Don't be thinking to
escape me now.   Rebellion is all one with witch-
craft, the ancient authors said that! (*Seizes and
pushes them into corner.*)

Widow Greely: Well now, Mayor Canavan, it
is you has gained great courage and great strength!

Canavan: Why wouldn't I have courage?   I
am Mayor of Scartana, I am safe from this out.
I am on the side of the strongest.   I am Mayor
in the Queen's service, and I have this shoe in
my hand!

> (*Enter Headley, his shoe hanging round his
> neck.   He has a gun in his hand, which
> he lays down.*)

Headley: Where is that pedlar?   I have
searched the Castle, he is not there.

Canavan: He came here out of the Castle, and
he is gone away out of this.

Headley: He did not lose much time.

Canavan: It was I hastened him.

Headley: You should have kept him.

Canavan: A worthless fellow!

Headley: A prize—did you hear what *she* said? (*Taps shoe.*)

Canavan: I did, well. (*Taps other shoe.*)

Headley: She said she would wish——

Canavan: The place left empty.

Headley: The deserter's head.

Canavan: I forgot that.

Headley: You told her he was a deserter.

Canavan: So he was, and a rebel.

Headley: She asked for his head to put under her royal feet.

Canavan: So she would, too, and she being without her shoes.

Headley: It would have been a love gift for me to proffer to her. I hurried back when I brought it to mind. I thought it would not take much time to whip off his head.

Canavan: I knew it was to be beheaded we were.

Headley: I have wasted time, I have lost half an hour, I have come back looking for a gift for my sovereign and you have thrown it away. (*He strikes Canavan with shoe.*)

Canavan: Stop railing at me and attacking me! I have a shoe of my own! (*Threatens him with it.*) I am grown now to be as brave as a lion!

Headley: (*Weeping.*)

It had been worth a ballad or a sonnet
To lay that head where she could step upon it!

Widow Deeny: His own kinsman's head.   But
he knows well what sort of a present would the
Queen like.

Widow Greely: Ah, what signifies one head to
her, unless it might belong to a bishop or a priest?

Widow Deeny: It is best for us to be going
home; it is milking time—but we might pick up
some little thing to bring along with us.   There
is a good ruff there on the hearth—   I suppose
it fell out of Antony's pack.

Widow Greely: There are more of his wearables
in the chimney (*She pulls down dress with tongs.*)—
very grand gaudy stuff indeed.   (*Feels it.*)

Headley: That dress!   What is it—what is
it (*Seizes it.*)—that dress, those flowers—that hem
—surely that is the hem that I kissed!

Widow Deeny: A nice broad hem it is, and well
sewed.

Headley: Get out of this, woman!   Leave that
alone!   That is no thing for you to handle!
(*Drives them out.*)

Widow Deeny: (*At door.*)   A very unmannerly
man!   (*They go out.*)

Headley: (*Pulling bodice down from chimney.*)
That silk—I am making no mistake—that ruff,
that headpiece—   What has happened—what

does it mean—there is no delusion—that *is* the
hem that I kissed.

Canavan: (*Who has sat down at table examining shoe.*) It is the right shoe is mine. Then
yours must be the left. It is the right should
mean the most share of favour.

Headley: (*Wildly.*) What is it has happened?
You were here—where is she? Where is the
Queen's Majesty—did you see her leave the room
in the Castle?

Canavan: What way would I see her? "Close
your eyes and your ears," she said, and I put
down my head in the bed. Would you think I
would break the first order she laid upon me?

Headley: But her dress is here—you must
know something——

Canavan: When I rose my head and looked
around, there was no sign of her at all, and I
made my way home. But quick as I was, that
lying rogue Antony was here before me.

Headley: What was he doing?

Canavan: He was thrusting something up
the chimney with the two hands of a tongs.

Headley: The Saints of Heaven preserve us!
What did he say?

Canavan: I asked him nothing, and he told
me nothing, unless lies. It was well to get quit
of him. He would be no sort of credit to a loyal
man at all.

Headley: (*Shaking him.*)   Don't you see what has happened?

Canavan: He has made off, and my joy be with him.

Headley: You were his abettor!

Canavan: A very unkind thing for you to say.

Headley: You are concealing his crime.

Canavan: Stop that, I will not be molested! I have the Queen's right shoe! I will not quail before any man!

Headley: You miserable villain! Don't you see I have discovered that your fellow criminal has killed the Queen!

Canavan: Killed the Queen is it?

Headley: You saw him hiding her dress in the chimney.

Canavan: I suppose that was it now.

Headley: He had made an end of her first!

Canavan: You say he did that?

Headley: He must have done it.

Canavan: Well now, that is a great overthrow!

Headley: What can he have done with the body? He could not have carried it down the Castle stairs?

Canavan: There was a rope from the window.

Headley: I saw it! A rope from the window, ribbons on it—it is certain he let down the body into the river!

Canavan: That was a good thought now.

Headley: There is a strong current in the stream that would sweep it away.

Canavan: Out into the sea. So it would too. It's with mermaids she'll be doing her travelling from this out, grabbing well-looking men from the rocks.

Headley: But her death will be heard of.

Canavan: It is certain it cannot be long hid.

Headley: The murderer will be searched for.

Canavan: He is safe enough, never fear.

Headley: Some one will be suspected. Essex will take revenge.

Canavan: He may not have the chance. It is not himself will be uppermost now, not having the support of the Queen.

Headley: You will be questioned—they will put you on the rack.

Canavan: They need not, I will tell all before the torture will begin.

Headley: They will say you did it. They will think you yourself have killed the Queen.

Canavan: What do you take me for? What an opinion you have of me! I would not take the credit from the man that deserves it, and that is my only brother, Antony Canavan!

Headley: You confess it was he did it?

Canavan: (*Examining clothes.*) I never thought now he would have the force to do a thing like

that, and she so fine a woman and he no great
hero of a man.

Headley: Was it done with a sword?

Canavan: A sword would be the quickest, I
would have heard a shot of a gun.

Headley: A stroke from behind?`

Canavan: No discredit if it was. It would
be very hard to stand up and to face a woman of
that sort.

Headley: To do it so quick!

Canavan: Within three minutes, I suppose,
of you yourself going out. Well, Antony Canavan, I never thought you would turn out so
great a man!

Headley: The black-hearted coward!

Canavan: Coward yourself! You yourself
kneeled to the Queen, and humbled yourself, and
cried for mercy. But my brother, without arms,
or help of soldiers, or troops at his call, or
meat in his stomach, it was he made an end
of her. A great man, a great man, there can be
no doubt at all of that!

Headley: You make a boast of it?

Canavan: Why would n't I make a boast and
he my own brother? Oh, he will leave a great
name after him in history! "Queen Elizabeth
was very strong," they will say, "she killed lords
and priests and bishops; but poor Antony Canavan
was stronger; it was he killed Queen Elizabeth!"

Headley: Oh, stop, stop! (*Puts hands over ears.*)

Canavan: I will be going now to join him. The whole country will be up supporting him. Essex did you say? Neither Essex nor another will dare let a squeak out of himself, before the man that made an end of the Queen!

Headley: You boasted of your loyalty!

Canavan: So I am loyal, to be sure. Loyal to the strongest, I always said I would be that. I have but one head only, and the place I will shelter it is under the strongest shelter to be had.

Headley: A terrible thought has come to me. Suppose, after all, the danger may fall upon me? It may be known it was to see myself she came!

Canavan: Don't be affrighted. I will protect you. Sure I said before you are of our own blood, a Canavan, Henry Canavan. Who would be safe if the kindred of Antony Canavan would not be safe?

Headley: Yes, yes, we are of one blood, but it would be better the crime not to be found out. I will destroy all the testimony. I will burn these clothes! (*Seizes dress.*)

Canavan: (*Stopping him.*) Quiet now and easy. There will be two words to that.

Headley: Her death cannot be hidden. But who can prove that she came to Scartana? Even Essex does not know that.

Canavan: Wait a while. I say these testimonies should be kept.

Headley: She said she kept her coming a secret.

Canavan: Just so. And I, being Antony's brother, they might not accept my witness.

Headley: They may think she was drowned crossing some stream.

Canavan: And the clergy would be taking the praise of it, saying they brought it about by their prayers.

Headley: Let them think Essex himself made away with her.

Canavan: So help me, no Englishman will ever take that credit to himself.

Headley: She had to pass many enemies.

Canavan: I wouldn't doubt O'Donnell to say he did it, or O'Neill to be claiming it for the North.

Headley: (*Putting dress and ruff on hearth.*) What can they accuse me of without evidence?

Canavan: It is I myself and Antony will carry the evidence through Munster! (*Takes dress off hearth, Headley puts it back.*) I will frustrate that! Antony will have it for a banner through the whole of the five provinces!

Headley: Give me the tinder-box. I will kindle the heap!

Canavan: Here is an answer to your kindling!

(*Takes water-jug and empties it on hearth.*) **Am** I going to allow evidence to be made away with by fire? It seems to me you are forgetting that I am Mayor of Scartana.

(*Enter the two widows.*)

Widow Greely: Take warning, Miller Canavan, your brother is coming against you with a pick.

Widow Deeny: To bring away your gold by force he is going, where you would not give it for his aid.

Widow Greely: Bad as you treated us a while ago, we would be loth to see a neighbour to be robbed.

(*Antony comes in with a pick, goes to board near door, and begins to rip it up.*)

Antony: This is the board where the widows said it was hid—the second board from the door. It is no robbery I to get what I was promised, and what I am in need of for a way of living.

(*Widows rush to stop him.*)

Widow Greely: Let you quit robbing the miller, I tell you, or I 'll have you scandalised through the town.

Canavan: Whisht your wordy mouth! Leave meddling with my brother!

Headley: Oh, he is tearing up a board! It is under that board he has the body buried! He is going to bring it away! Oh, I will not

see it! I will not look at those royal blood-
stains on that pearl-white neck! Oh, it would
haunt me, it would start me in a faint! No,
no, I will not look! (*Turns away and hides his
face in ruff.*)

Antony: (*Shaking off Canavan.*) I got the
promise, and I will bring away my share of
money in spite of you!

Canavan: Oh, Antony, my dear brother,
take it! Take all that I have!

Antony: (*Taking a bag from under board.*)
I 'll get handsome work now! I 'm thankful to
you, Peter. It 's a wonder you to have turned
kind.

Canavan: Ah, why would n't I be kind after
the kindness you have showed to the whole
nation? Take my cloak now, and my chain
to put around your neck!

Antony: It 's not an hour hardly since I
was a ragtail, and a fly-swarm, and a rebel, and
a breaker of the laws!

Canavan: You can make new laws yourself
now for the good of the whole nation!

Antony: You drove me out, where I would
not swear to the Queen!

Canavan: What ailed you not telling me you
had done better than to swear to her? Take
it, take it, take all my treasure and my gold!
You will want it, you will want it for the

suit a general should wear! All that I have is yours! You are my only brother! I am proud of you, Antony Canavan, for the deed you have done this day! (*Hugs him.*)

Headley: Is he gone? Has he the body carried away? No, but he is there still! Wretch! Monster! Traitor! Rebel! I will not leave you living! (*Draws sword and rushes at him.*)

Widow Greely: (*Seizing him.*) Whatever Antony Canavan may have done, I will not let a Queen's man attack him.

Widow Deeny: The Queen's army to make an attack on him, we are sure he has done some good thing!

Canavan: Bad cess to you, Henry Canavan! Let you quit making that assault. Tie him to the chair. I 'll learn him manners! I 'll learn him to attack my only brother! (*He and the widows overcome Headley and tie him to chair. Canavan and Antony kneel down by board searching for more money.*)

Headley: Send me back to Lord Essex! It is as well for me go confess all. "She is dead," I will say, "it is my fault, it was on my account she came here, on the head of my features and my face. Disfigure my face," I will say. "Destroy my beauty, strike off the hand that wrote the verses that brought the queen to her death!"

Widow Greely: Brought her to her death! Are you in earnest saying the Queen was brought to her death?

Headley: It is true, it is true. But it was that traitor Antony that killed her, it was he struck that wicked blow.

Antony: (*Making ready to go.*) I wonder, Peter, for what length of time should I be a miller before I 'd get the name of a hare's heart like your own?

Widow Greely: You to have a hare's heart! The heart of a roadside gander, and it defending its brood!

Widow Deeny: The heart of a horned heifer, its first calf being brought away!

Canavan: The candle of bravery and courage you are, the tower of the western world! Oh, my comely Antony, it is to you I will give the branch!

Antony: Have you a mind to destroy me and to shorten my days? Let ye stop, I say, from praising me and from putting up my name.

Canavan: Bashful he is, no way high in himself, as bashful and as humble as a child of two years! I tell you, Antony Canavan, it is you are the pride of your race!

Widow Greely: Our blessing for ever on the man that put terror on the heart of the tyrant!

Widow Deeny: A shout on the three heights of Ireland for the mightiest hero of the Gael! (*They shout and with Canavan begin to dance slowly round him.*)

Antony: What at all are you doing? What at all have you against me? Is it to destroy me you would, putting a big name on me to lead me to my death? (*They shout "Hi for Antony."*) Is there no one at all in the whole country to shout for that you must go shouting for myself? You to have done that, I am a gone man. It is my grave every shout is digging in the clay, and it 's boards for my burying you are readying with your dance. It would be as well for me to go out, and meet my death in some fight.

Canavan: To fight is it? There will be no fighting where you will be, and where myself will be! The enemy will run before us the same as long-tailed lambs! It is the sight of my brave Antony will set them flocking into the tide!

Widow Deeny: (*Looking out of door.*) Oh, let you look! A troop of soldiers and Lord Essex at the head of them! They are passing down the road by the mill-stream!

Antony: (*Sits down beside Headley.*) So long as you are all joined in a league for to bring about my death, I will wait for it here and now. There is no use at all trying to escape a prophecy.

Give me your hand, Henry Canavan, it is the one blow might put an end to the two of us.

Headley: (*Clinging to him.*) It is happy for the widows spinning wool and flax and tow, and that never went knocking about among the great ones of the earth. It would be best for the two of us, Antony, we never to have laid an eye at all on the Queen, as it is little she served us in the end.

Widow Greely: Will you look at the pair of them trembling, as weak as water and as pale! It is you yourself, Miller Canavan, is the hardiest in the house at this time.

Canavan: (*Seizing gun.*) Ha! Is that so? So it is too. Queen Elizabeth was strong, Antony Canavan was stronger—what is he now beside me? Wait now till I have my eye cocked to take aim at Lord Essex and his men! (*Takes aim out of door.*)

Widow Deeny: Do not be so daring, to destroy the whole army, and you without protection unless it is the thatch above your head.

Canavan: Little I care for them! I 'm as venturesome as a robin in the snow! I would fire, and it to bring earthquakes! (*Fires off gun from door, and falls back from kick of gun. Widows shriek as he fires, then look cautiously out.*)

Widow Greely: We are as good as dead this time anyway.

Widow Deeny: No, but taking off his hat Lord Essex is, and saluting the miller as he goes.

Antony: A salute to himself he thought it to be, there being no bullet in the gun.

Canavan: (*Looking out of door.*) To take off his hat he did! To bow and to bare his head he did! To bid his men hasten their horses he did, and to run before myself and my gun! (*Turns and holds out his arm over Headley and Antony.*) Let you not be daunted! It is I will protect the whole of ye! Where is fear? It is banished from the world from this day! The strongest! Is n't it the fool I was wasting time—wasting the years— looking here and there for the strongest? I give you my word, it was not till this present minute that I knew the strongest to be myself!

Curtain

THE WHITE COCKADE

TO R. G., SCENE PAINTER

PERSONS

Patrick Sarsfield   .   .   .   EARL OF LUCAN

King James II.

Carter .   .   .   SECRETARY TO KING JAMES

A Poor Lady

Matt Kelleher OWNER OF AN INN AT DUNCANNON

Mary Kelleher . . . . . HIS WIFE

Owen Kelleher . . . . . . HIS SON

First Sailor

Second Sailor

First Williamite

Second Williamite

A Captain and other Williamites

Act I

Scene: An Inn kitchen at Duncannon. Owen Kelleher lying on the hearth playing jackstones. Mrs. Kelleher rubbing a bit of meat. A barrel beside her.

Owen: One—and one—and five—that's scatters.

Mrs. Kelleher: Leave playing jackstones, Owen, and give me a hand salting the meat.

Owen: Two — and two — and one — that's doubles. There is time enough. Sure it's not to-day it's wanted.

Mrs. Kelleher: What's put off till harvest is put off for ever. It's best to catch the pig by the leg when you get her. The French ship might be going before we have the barrels ready, and some other might get the profit.

Owen: The ship didn't get orders yet from King James. The sailors were not sure was it to Dublin he would bid them go, or to some other place. It is time for us to be hearing news of him. I have a mind to go ask it.

Mrs. Kelleher: Come over and rub a bit of

77

the meat, and leave thinking about King James. We hear enough talk of him, listening to poor Lady Dereen.

Owen: You have not enough of salt to pack the meat till my father will bring it back from Ross.

Mrs. Kelleher: The lamb teaching its mother to bleat! If I have not itself, I have what serves for rubbing it. (*She pushes back dresser from before a side door.*) Be moving now, and come down to the cellar till we bring up another leg of the pork.

Owen: (*Going on playing.*) One—and one—and one—crow's nest.

Mrs. Kelleher: (*Going through door to cellar.*) I give you my word it is as hard to make you stir as to make a hedgehog run.

(*Owen whistles "The White Cockade."*)

Mrs. Kelleher: (*Coming back with another bit of meat.*) It is yourself finds the hob a good harbourage!

Owen: It is not worth my while to be bringing it up bit by bit—if it was to bring up the whole of it now——

Mrs. Kelleher: I suppose not! I wonder now what is worth your while if it is not to mind the place and the inn that will be coming to yourself some day. It is a poor hen that can't scratch for itself!

Owen: There might be something worth doing outside this place.

Mrs. Kelleher: (*Scornfully.*) There might! It's the hills far off that are green!

Owen: It is beyond the hills I would like to be going. There is no stir at all in this place.

Mrs. Kelleher: What is it at all you are wanting or talking about?

Owen: There is fighting going on through the country.

Mrs. Kelleher: And for all the profit it will bring ourselves it might be the fighting of the hornless cows! It is best for us to be minding our own business.

Owen: There used to be great fighters in Ireland in the old times.

Mrs. Kelleher: If there were, they had no other trade! Every crane according to its thirst. Believe me, if they had found as good a way of living as what you have, they would not have asked to go rambling. I know well it is an excuse you are making, with your talk of fighting and your songs, not to be doing the work that is at your hand. You are as lazy as the tramp that will throw away his bag. You would have got the sluggard's prize from Aristotle of the books!

Owen: Well, it's good to be best at something.

Mrs. Kelleher: If you saw a car and horse

coming at you, you would not stir out of the
rut! You would spend your night on the floor
sooner than go up a ladder to the loft! Stir!
You would not stir yourself to turn the crispy
side of a potato if you had but the one bite only!

Owen: One—and four—high castles.

Mrs. Kelleher: I tell you a day will come
when you will grow to the ground the way you
never will reach to heaven!

Owen: It is time for you to leave off faulting
me. There is some one coming to the door.

Mrs. Kelleher: (*Looking out of door.*) It is
the poor Lady. She wasn't here this good
while. It is a pity she to have gone spending
all for the King the way she did, and to go
in beggary and misery ever after. (*Owen sings*)—

> The cuckoo has no word to say,
> Sharp grief has put us under rent,
> The heavy cloud is on the Gael,
> But comely James will bring content!

Mrs. Kelleher: I believe it is herself put the
half of those songs in your head. (*Pulls dresser
over door.*) It is best shut this door. There
is no use too many eyes seeing it.

> (*Old Lady comes in. Her hand is over her
> eyes as if half blind. She wears ragged
> clothes that have once been handsome.*)

Mrs. Kelleher: You are welcome, my poor Lady Dereen.

Lady: I thank you, Mary Kelleher. I have always found a welcome in this house, and a shelter from the heat and the rain.

Mrs. Kelleher: Who should get a welcome here if you would n't get it, Lady? And I born and reared on your own estate before you lost it through the wars.

Lady: I have had great losses, but now I will have great gains. I lost all through Charles; I will get all back through James. My eyes are tired watching for the sun to rise in the east. The sun of our success is rising at last!

Mrs. Kelleher: It is time for success to come to yourself, Lady, indeed. I remember the time you had great riches.

Lady: I did not grudge anything, my lord did not grudge anything to Charles Stuart, our King. I shall be rich again now; I never lost my faith.

Mrs. Kelleher: Well, I would never have faith myself in the thing I would n't see.

Lady: I lost all through Charles; I will get all back through James!

Mrs. Kelleher: That you may, Lady. I would sooner you to have kept it when you had it. A wren in the fist is better than a crane on loan. It 's hard getting butter out of a dog's mouth.

Lady: The Stuart has been under the mists

of night.   The sun is rising that will scatter
them.   The whole country is going out to help
him.   The young men are leaving the scythes in
the meadows; the old men are leaving the sta-
tions and the blessed wells.   Give me some white
thing—some feathers—I have to make cockades
for the King's men.

Mrs. Kelleher: (*Giving her feathers from the
dresser.*)   Look at that now!   These come as
handy as a gimlet.   I was plucking ducks yesterday for the captain of the French ship.

Lady: (*Taking feathers and beginning to fasten
them together with shaking hands.*)   James, our own
King, will bring prosperity to us all.

Mrs. Kelleher: So long as we get it, I would n't
mind much what King brings it.   One penny
weighs as good as another, whatever King may
have his head upon it.   If you want to grow
old, you must use hot and cold.

Lady: Is it nothing to you, Mary Kelleher, that
the broken altars of the Faith will be built up
again?

Mrs. Kelleher: God grant it!   Though, indeed, myself I am no great bigot.   I would always
like to go to a Protestant funeral.   You would
see so many well-dressed people at it.

Lady: (*Beginning to make another cockade.*)   I
must be quick, very quick.   There will be a hard
battle fought.   William, the Dutchman, has

brought trained men from all the countries of
Europe. James has gone out to meet him.

Mrs. Kelleher: Is it going to fight a battle he
is? It is likely he will have sent orders to the
French ship, so. It is to take his orders it was
here. The dear knows where it might be to-
morrow, and the pigs we have killed left on our
hands! Only for you giving me no help the way
you did, Owen, the meat would be nearer ready
now than what it is. Look at him now, Lady;
maybe he 'll mind what you will say. Bid
him leave lying on the floor at midday.

Lady: It is time you should get up, boy;
there is plenty of work to do.

Mrs. Kelleher: That is what I am saying.
Work for all hands.

Lady: Work for all, and no time to lose.

Mrs. Kelleher: That is what I am saying.
What is put off till harvest——

Lady: It is not right for a young man with
strong hands to be taking his ease. (*Owen gets
up and stands awkwardly.*)

Mrs. Kelleher: And his mother not sparing
herself.

Lady: You lying there, while there is a friend
out under the heat of the day fighting our battle.

Mrs. Kelleher: My poor man! So he is. Striving to bring the salt.

Lady: (*Giving Owen a cockade.*) Take that

White Cockade. Go out, go northward. Join the King's army, go and fight for the King!

Mrs. Kelleher: To fight for the King, is it?

Lady: Hurry, hurry, you may be in time to strike a blow for him! (*Sings with a feeble voice*)—

> Our heart's desire, our pleasant James,
> Our treasure and our only choice!

Mrs. Kelleher: Look here now, Lady, have sense. I have but the one son only, and is it sending him away from me you would be?

Lady: Our King has no son; he has false daughters. We must give our sons to the King!

Mrs. Kelleher: It is my opinion we must keep them to mind ourselves. What profit would he get joining the King's army? It is not the one thing to go to town and come from it.

Lady: (*Putting hand on her arm.*) It would be a pity to disappoint so great a friend.

Mrs. Kelleher: That is true, but reason is reason. I have but the one son to help me; and it is what I say: you can't whistle and eat oatmeal; the gull can't attend the two strands; words won't feed the friars. How will Owen mind this place, and he maybe shot as full of holes as a riddle?

Owen: When you have your minds made up if it's to go fighting I am, or to go rubbing the

bacon I am, it will be time enough for me **to**
stir myself.

Lady: Do you grudge your service? Will you
betray the King as the English betrayed him?
O my heart leaps up with my pleasant Stuart!

Owen: I would like well to go serve the
King; but I don't know how could I do it.

Lady: You say that because of idleness. It
is through idleness you have come ˌto have a
coward's heart, the heart of a linnet, of a trader,
a poor, weak spirit, a heart of rushes.

Mrs. Kelleher: You are too hard now, Lady,
upon the boy. Leave him alone. There is no
man knows which is best, hurry or delay. It's
often it's not better to be first than last.
Many a tattered colt makes a handsome horse.
The first thread is not of the piece. It's not
the big men cut all the harvest. When the time
comes, the child comes. Every good comes by
waiting.

Lady: King James in the country wanting all
his helpers!

Mrs. Kelleher: Let every herring hang by its
own tail.

Lady: It is for our comfort he has come.

Mrs. Kelleher: He might. It's to please itself
the cat purrs.

Lady: (*Putting hand on Owen's shoulder.*) The
Stuart in the field!

Mrs. Kelleher: (*Seizing other shoulder.*) The meat in the cellar!

Lady: Our hero in danger!

Mrs. Kelleher: Our bacon in danger!

Lady: Our prince under mists!

Mrs. Kelleher: Our meat under mildew!

Lady: Oh! The great Stuart!

Mrs. Kelleher: (*Striking it.*) The empty barrel!

> (*Owen turns from one to the other, undecided.
> Voices are heard singing a French song.*)

Lady: Is that the army of the King?

Mrs. Kelleher: It is what is worse. It's the French sailors coming for the meat and it not ready.

> (*Two sailors come in singing*)—

> Madame, si vous voulez danser
> Vite je vous prie de commencer
> Avec l'air des Français,
> Avec l'air de la Cour.

First Sailor: We are come, Madame, for the pork and the bacon.

Second Sailor: And de sau-sa-ges.

Mrs. Kelleher: I haven't them ready yet.

First Sailor: We must sail this night before morning.

Mrs. Kelleher: Did you get any orders from King James?

First Sailor: We did not get them. He is fighting in the north, at some river. We go to Dublin. If he succeed, we carry news to France. If he is beaten, he will want help from France. We sail at sunrise when the tide is high.

Mrs. Kelleher: Well, look now; I will have the meat for you before that.

First Sailor: All right. There is moon. We will come to the pier before sunrise, after the midnight.

Mrs. Kelleher: There is a quick way. Maybe you don't know the outer door to the cellar?

Second Sailor: I do know it. I did put wine in there last week—no duty; no douane. (*Puts finger on nose.*)

(*Matt Kelleher comes bursting in. He throws a bag of salt on the floor.*)

Mrs. Kelleher: Here is himself, and he running like a hare before hounds. Give me here the salt.

Matt: Salt! salt! salt! Who would be talking of salt?

Mrs. Kelleher: The ship is going.

Matt: Where is the use of salt on such a day as this, unless it might be to make a man drouthy?

Mrs. Kelleher: I tell you I was as idle without it as a smith without bellows.

Matt: To make a man drouthy! To give him

a good thirst, the way he will drink to the King.

Mrs. Kelleher: Indeed, if signs are signs, I think you yourself have been drinking to the King!

Matt: We will all drink to the King! Where are the glasses?

Mrs. Kelleher: Quiet yourself now. You are too good a customer to yourself; putting on the mill the straw of the kiln.

Matt: Would you begrudge me so much as one glass on a day like this?

Mrs. Kelleher: What has happened on this day more than any other day?

Matt: This day has brought news of the battle, I tell you—of the great battle at the Boyne!

First Sailor: The Boyne—that is it! That is the same story we heard.

Matt: Where would you hear your story? It was away in Ross I got mine. There was news brought to the barracks there.

Mrs. Kelleher: Tell me now, was the battle fought in earnest?

Matt: Fought is it? It is it that was fought! A great battle—the ground that was hard turning soft, and the ground that was soft turning hard, under the trampling of feet! The sea coming in on the land, and the land going out into the sea! Fire from the edges of every sword! The blood falling like a shower in harvest time! The air black with ravens; the river reddened with blood! Sarsfield going through the field the same as fire through furze.

Mrs. Kelleher: What there is good comes out in the blood. Sure he is of the race of Conall Cearnach. What would an apple be like but an apple? What would the cat's son do but kill mice?

Matt: King James raging like a lion in every gap!

Lady: Oh! I knew it! I knew it! The brave Stuart!

Mrs. Kelleher: And who was it, will you tell me, that won in the fight?

Matt: Sure, am n't I telling you, if you would listen? The man has won that should win, great King James!

Lady: I knew the sun would rise at last for victory!

Matt: You will get your rights now, **Lady**. We 'll all get our rights. (*Sings*) —

> Three times the fairest of the Scots,
> The blossomed branch, the Phœnix rare,
> Our secret love, our only choice,
> The shining candle of the war!

Lady: My lord spent all upon Charles. James will pay all back again!

Matt: He will, he will! You will get your estates, Lady, and your white halls! We will drink the cellar dry the day you get your estates. There will be red wine of Spain running through your white halls!

Lady: I have his promise! I have the King's seal to his promise!

> (*She takes a large seal and folded parchment from a bag hanging at her side and shows it.*)

Matt: It is a good seal—a grand seal. Drink a health, I say, to the King's seal! Let me go down to the cellar for spirits—no, but for wine!

> (*He pushes back dresser. Mrs. Kelleher pulls him from the door.*)

Mrs. Kelleher: You will not go down. Thirst makes thirst!

Matt: (*To sailors.*) Go down there, I say. Bring up a bottle—two bottles—plenty of bottles!   (*They go down.*)

Lady: I will go to Dublin. I will go to his Court. I will show him the promise and the seal.

Matt: You will, ma'am. He can't deny the seal.

Lady: I will put on my silks and my velvets. I will have jewels about my neck. I will bid my waiting-women to spread out my dress. (*Makes a gesture as if spreading out a train.*)

Matt: It is you will look well, Lady, as you did in the old times, with your silks and your jewels.

Lady: I will come to the door. The coach will stop—the young lords will hand me out of it—my own young kinsmen will be there.

Matt: I will go see you in the coach, Lady. It is I myself will open the door!

Lady: They will bring me to the throne-room. I will leave my cloak at the door. I will walk up to the throne! (*She walks a few steps.*)

Matt: (*Walking crookedly.*) I will walk up myself. I would like well to see the King on his throne.

Lady: (*Curtsying.*) A curtsy to the right to the Queen—a curtsy to the left to the princesses.

Matt: (*Curtsying.*) That is it, that is it! We will curtsy to the princesses.

Lady: The King will smile at me. I will take out the King's seal. (*Touches it.*) I will kneel and kiss his hand.

Matt: I will kneel—no, I will not. (*Stumbles and kneels.*) There, I did now in spite of myself. Here, Mary, help me up again.

Mrs. Kelleher: Stop where you are, Kelleher, and be ashamed of yourself. When wine goes in, wit goes out.

Owen: (*Helping the lady up.*) All will go

well with you now, Lady, since the King has
gained the day.

Mrs. Kelleher: Maybe he was not the winner
after all. It is often we heard news from Ross
that would n't be true after.

Matt: Why would n't he win? He has the
prayers of the people with him.

Lady: He has God with him.

Owen: He has Sarsfield with him.

Lady: Oh! who will go to the King? who
will go for news of the King?

Owen: I will go.

Lady: Yes, go, go! Here, take these to give
to the King's men. (*She gives him cockades.*)

Mrs. Kelleher: Do not go until we are sure
is the battle over. The last of a feast is better
than the first of a fight.

Owen: I will go now. I delayed long enough.
I wish I had gone in time for the fighting.

Mrs. Kelleher: Well, since he is the winner
—a friend in Court is better than a coin in the
pocket—it might be for profit.

> (*Owen begins washing hands and face in
> a basin. Puts on coat. Sailors bring
> up an armful of bottles from cellar.*)

Matt: (*Still on the floor, seizing a bottle.*)
Here 's to the King's health, I say!

> (*The sailors give him glasses; he opens bottle,
> fills them, and they hand them round.*)

Lady: (*Touching glass with her lips, and throwing it down.*)   The King and the King's right!

Mrs. Kelleher: The King and the Catholics in   fashion!

Owen: The King that fought the battle!

Sailors: The King and France!

Matt: The King and wine without duty!

All together: King James and Ireland!

All: (*Singing*)—

O well-tuned harp of silver strings,
O strong green oak, O shining Mars,
Our hearts' desire, fair James our King,
Our great Cuchulain in the war!

Curtain

Act II

Scene I

Scene: A wood. James sitting on a camp stool. He is richly dressed, and wears an Order. Carter standing beside him. Sarsfield pointing with sword to a map on the ground.

Sarsfield: If your Majesty will look at the plan I have marked on this map, you will see how we can make up for the defeat of the Boyne. The news we have had of William's march makes it very simple. He will be in our hands by morning. You know what we have to do to-night. To morrow we shall be dictating terms from Limerick.

James: Yes, yes, you told me all that. I wonder if this wood is quite safe. (*Looks round.*)

Sarsfield: If our army had to fall back, it fell back in good order. We have guns, stores, horses. We have plenty of troops to strengthen Athlone. We can keep the mass of the enemy from passing the Shannon.

James: I hope the bridge we crossed that last little river by has been broken so that no one can follow us.

Sarsfield: Kilkenny must be strengthened too. Waterford is loyal. Munster and Connacht are safe. Our success will give us back Dublin. In half an hour our horses will be rested. We must be at Clonmel before midnight.

James: But there is a troop of William's men somewhere about. We might fall into their hands.

Sarsfield: They are in small divisions. We and our few men will be more than a match for them.

James: Of course, of course; but we must not risk our lives.

Carter: Not a doubt of it! The King's life must not be put in danger!

Sarsfield: Danger! Who says that? Who said it at the Boyne? Was it you drove the King from the battle? Bad advisers! Bad advisers! He who says "danger" is a bad adviser.

Carter: I did nothing—it was His Majesty's own doing.

James: Yes, yes, of course. I am more than a soldier. I have the whole kingdom to think of.

Carter: Not a doubt of it. But you and I, Sarsfield, have only ourselves to think of.

Sarsfield: You and I—may be—this dust (*Striking himself*)—that dust of yours—has the

King's livery made us of the one baking? No, no;
there is some leaven in this dough. (*To the King.*)
Rouse yourself, sir.   Put your hand to the work.

James: I suppose I must carry out this
plan of a surprise.

Sarsfield: That is right, sir.   Carry it out
and the Boyne will be forgotten.

James: Is that some noise?   (*Starts.*)

Sarsfield: It is but the trampling of our own
horses.

James: Just go, Sarsfield, and see to the
breaking of that bridge. If we are caught
here by those murderous Dutch, your plans
will be ended with a rope or a scaffold.

Sarsfield: I will send orders on to Clonmel.
The Boyne will be forgotten!—forgotten!

(*Goes out.*)

James: I hope Sarsfield knows what he
is talking about.

Carter: H'm—he may.

James: If we are sure of winning——

Carter: Just so.

James: He says we are sure.

Carter: He does.

James: I hope there will be not much more
fighting.

Carter: Or any.

James: That would be best; if they would
give in without a fight.

Carter: Best, indeed.

James: But if there is danger——

Carter: There is always danger.

James: Of another battle——

Carter: Or a surprise.

James : I would prefer to be elsewhere. It is all very well for those who have a taste for fighting. I had it once myself—when I was a boy. But it has gone from me now with the taste for green apples.

Carter: Not a doubt of it.

James: A king's life does not belong to himself.

Carter: He must not let it be taken.

James: He must not let it be risked.

Carter: That is what I meant.

James: Now if we had come to the sea——

Carter: We would be handy to it.

James: If there were a French ship——

Carter: And a fair wind.

James: We might—what is that?

  (*Owen's voice heard singing "The White Cockade."*)

Carter: It is a friend—he is singing "The White Cockade."

Owen: (*Comes in singing*)—

The heavy cloud is on the Gael,
But comely James will bring content.

James: Where are you going, boy?

Owen: I am going looking for news of King James. (*Sits down and wipes his face.*) I'm after wringing my shirt twice, with respects to you. I would not have walked so far for any one living but the King! And it is bad news of him I am after getting.

James: Then the defeat is known. What did you hear?

Owen: I heard a great clattering of horses, and then I heard a fife and drum—a tune they were playing like this.

(*Whistles "Lillibulero."*)

James : The rebels are here! It is "Lillibulero"!

Owen: Then I saw a troop of men and of horses.

James: Were they Dutch?

Owen: They were not. They were as good speakers as myself. Men from the north they were, and they were giving out as they passed that William had gained the day, and that King James was running, and if they got him, they would give his legs rest for a while.

James: Heavens! What a terrible threat!

Carter: Terrible, indeed! Is there no place where we could be safe?

Owen: If you belong to King James, you would be safe where I come from, and that is the inn at the harbour of Duncannon.

James: The harbour! Do many ships come in there?

Owen: There do not. But there is one in it presently.

James: An English ship?

Owen: It is not, but a ship from France. But if it is itself, it is not long it will be in it. It will be sailing at sunrise. There will be a boat coming from it after midnight, for the meat my mother has them promised.

James: I must go to Duncannon! Look here, boy, would it be safe if I—if the King himself were to go there to-night?

Owen: Now that he is down, I think there is not one in the place but would carry a hurt dog if it belonged to King James.

James: But tell me—if—I only say *if* the King should come and should be seen by anyone—is there any chance he would be known?

Owen: Every chance. Sure he is well known by the songs.

James: By the songs?

Owen: (*Singing*)—

Curled locks like Angus of the Sidhe,
Friendly, brave, bright, loving, fair;
High hawk that gains the mastery,
Cupid in peace, a Mars in war!

James: (*To Carter.*) It will be safer not to

go till after dark. We must go quite quietly—
we must leave our men and horses at a dis-
tance.

Carter: That will be best.

James : You must keep the inn clear, boy.
You must keep the French boat till I come—
till the King comes. He will knock at the door
before midnight.

Owen: Believe me he will get a good welcome!
If it was known he was coming there would be a
candle lighted in every harbour.

James: No, no candles.

Owen: I may as well be going now to make
all ready. (*Goes out singing*)–

> Three times the fairest of the Scots,
> My prince and my heart-secret, James,
> Our treasure and our only choice—
> The darling Cæsar of the Gael!

James: That was a good chance. We can go
on board at once, and slip away to France. I
have done with this detestable Ireland.

(Kicks the ground.)

Carter: And I.   (*Kicks the ground.*)

James: It might be as well——

Carter: Well?

James: Not to mention anything——

Carter: I won't

James: That is, nothing more than the sending of despatches to—here he is coming.

(*Puts his finger to his lips. Carter nods. Sarsfield comes in.*)

Sarsfield: I have sent orders to Clonmel, sir. A thousand of our men will have gathered there to meet us at midnight.

James: I have changed my mind. I have had messages. I knew France would not desert me. There is a ship at Duncannon. I have despatches to send to King Louis. I will go to Duncannon to-night, and not to Clonmel.

Sarsfield: We cannot afford that delay, sir. We should lose the chance of surprising the Dutch troop.

James: That is enough, General Sarsfield. You will obey orders.

Sarsfield: Are they, sir, what is best for Ireland?

James: Yes, yes, of course. She is a very good rod to beat England with.

Sarsfield: Whatever use you may put her to, sir, you are bound to do your best for her now.

James: Yes, yes, of course.

Sarsfield: The troops coming to us must not be left to scatter again. They believe yet in the King. They are sure he will not betray them again——

James: I am not betraying them. I am get-

ting them help from France. You need say
no more. When I think well of fighting I will
fight; when I think well of retreating I will
retreat.

> (*He walks to end of stage and looks at
> himself in a hand-mirror.*)

Carter: Not a doubt of it! I hope General
Sarsfield will loyally follow your Majesty's orders.

Sarsfield: Obey them? And what about Ireland—the lasting cry? Am I giving heed to the
lasting cry of luckless Ireland? Am I listening
to that?

Carter: You have sworn to obey the King.

Sarsfield: Just so, just so, we have sworn.—
He is our King—we have taken the oath. Well,
is not a feather in a hat as good a cry as
another? A feather in a hat, a King in a song:

> The darling Cæsar of the Gael,
> The great Cuchulain of the War!

(*Fife and drum heard playiug "Lillibulero."*)

James: (*Rushing back.*) That is Lillibulero!
Oh, the rebels are coming!

Sarsfield: It is that troop we knew of. They
are not many. We have enough men to stand
against them.   (*Music heard, right.*)

James: They are coming very close!

Carter: Here, sir, let us hide in the wood!

> (*They run left.*)

James: They are coming this way!
(*They cross to right.   Music follows.*)
Carter: Is it an army or an echo?
(*They run left again.*)
James: (*Clinging to Sarsfield.*)   It is all around us!

Sarsfield: (*Taking up cloak which James has dropped.*)   I can offer your Majesty's ears the protection of this cloak.   (*Holds out cloak over them, as music dies away.*)

Scene II

Scene: Inn kitchen, much as before, but without the barrel; night-time, candles burning.   Owen standing as if just come in.   Matt and Mrs. Kelleher with back to audience listening to him. Old Lady sitting, her head in her hands, rocking herself.

Mrs. Kelleher: The King beaten!   Sure they said first he had won.   Well, the bottom comes out of every riddle at the last!

Matt: I had it in my mind there was some great misfortune coming upon us.   I was trying to hearten myself through the whole of the morning. I give you my word, now, I am as sorry as if there was one dead belonging to me!

Owen: Did you hear me, Lady, what I was telling?

Lady: (*Sitting up.*)   If it was trúe, it was a dark story, a dark sorrowful story!

   (*She gets up and looks out of door into the darkness.*)

Owen: King James is beaten surely.

Lady: The King beaten, and the moon in the skies not darkened!

Owen: Beaten and wandering.

Lady: The King beaten, and the fish not dead in the rivers!

Owen: Beaten and wandering and hunted.

   (*Matt Kelleher gives a groan at the end of each sentence.*)

Lady: The King beaten, and the leaves on the trees not withered!   (*She turns from the door.*) The sun is a liar that rose in the east for victory. What was the sun doing that day?   Where was God?   Where was Sarsfield?

   (*She walks up and down, wringing her hands.*)

Mrs. Kelleher: It is what I was often saying, there is nought in this world but a mist.

Lady: Where were the people that were wise and learned?   Where were the troop readying their spears?   Where are they till they smooth out this knot for me?   (*Takes Owen by the shoulders.*)   Why did not the hills fall upon the traitors?   Why did not the rivers rise against them?

Mrs. Kelleher: Sit down now, Lady, for a while. It 's no wonder you to be fretting, and your lands and your means gone like froth on the stream. Sure the law of borrowing, is the loan to be broken.

Lady: I will not sit under a roof and my King under clouds. It is not the keening of one plain I hear, but of every plain. The sea and the waves crying through the harbour! The people without a lord but the God of glory! Where is he? Where is my royal Stuart? I will go out crying after the King! (*She goes out.*)

Mrs. Kelleher: But is it surely true, Owen, that the King is coming to this house?

Owen: Sure and certain sure.

Mrs. Kelleher: If we had but known, to have killed a sheep or a kid itself! I declare I would think more of him now than when he had all at his command.

Owen: It is likely, indeed, he found no good table in the wood.

Mrs. Kelleher: The man without dinner is two to supper. Well, the cakes are baked, and eggs we have in plenty, and pork if we had but the time to boil it, and a bit of corned beef. Indeed if I had twenty times as much, I would n't begrudge it to the King.

Matt: (*Looking at bottles.*) There is good wine for him anyway. The Frenchmen knew the best corner.

Mrs. Kelleher: Mind yourself, now.

Matt: (*Indignantly.*) Do you think I would take so much as one drop from what I have put on one side for the rightful King?

Mrs. Kelleher: Give me a hand to get down the best delft. It's well I had the barrels packed out of the way. It's getting on for midnight. He might be here any time.

(*Trampling of horses heard, and fife and drum playing "Lillibulero.")*

Matt: What is that? Is it the King that is coming?

Owen: It is not; but King William's men that are looking for the King.

Mrs. Kelleher: Keep them out of this! Foxes in the hencoop!

Owen: It is here they are coming, sure enough.

(*Music comes nearer. Mrs. Kelleher hurriedly puts food in cupboard and flings a sack over bottles. Door is opened; two men of William's army come in. They have fife and drum.*)

First Williamite: That is good! I smell supper.

Second Williamite: We are lucky to find an inn so handy.

First Williamite: I knew where the inn was. I told the Newry troop to come meet us here. (*Turns to door.*) Here, you lads, go and spread yourselves here and there through the town:

don't go far; I will fire two shots when you are wanted. (*Voices outside.*) "All right." "We 'll do that, sir."

Second Williamite: I don't think King James is in these parts at all.

First Williamite: There is a French ship in the harbour. He might be making for her.

Second Williamite: We will stop here anyway. We have a good view of the pier in the moonlight.

Mrs. Kelleher: I am loath to disoblige you, gentlemen, but you can't stop here to-night.

First Williamite: Why do you say that? Inns were made to stop in.

Mrs. Kelleher: This is not an inn now—not what you would rightly call an inn — we gave up business of late—we were stumbling under the weight of it, like two mice under a stack.

First Williamite: I wouldn't think so small a place would be so great a burden.

Mrs. Kelleher: A hen itself is heavy if you carry it far. It 's best to give up in time. A good run is better than a bad battle. We got no comfort for ourselves—who is nearest the church is not nearest the altar.

First Williamite: Quiet this woman, some of you. Where is the man of the house? The hen does n't crow when there is a cock in the yard— you see, ma'am, I have proverbs myself.

Mrs. Kelleher: (*To Matt.*) We must keep

them out some way. (*To Williamites.*) There
are no beds for you to get. The beds are damp.
Are n't they, Matt?

Matt: Damp, indeed—rotten with damp.

Owen: Damp and soaked with the drip from
the roof.

First Williamite: Beds! Are we asking for
beds? It is not often we feel a blanket over us,
thanks to King James. These chairs will do us
well.

Mrs. Kelleher: You don't know what lay on
those chairs last night!

First Williamite: What was that?

Mrs. Kelleher: A corpse—was n't it, Matt?

Matt: It was—a dead corpse.

Owen: Cold and dead.

First Williamite: (*Contemptuously.*) Corpses!
I was own brother to a corpse in the last scrim-
mage. A knock I got on the head. Sit down.

Mrs. Kelleher: It is likely you don't know
what sickness did this one die of. Of a small-
pox—did n't it, Matt?

Matt: It did. Of a pitted small-pox.

Owen: And it left lying there without a coffin.

First Williamite: It would be worse news if
it had got a wake that had left the house bare.

Mrs. Kelleher: Bare! This is the house
that is bare! I have a bad husband, have n't I,
Matt?

Matt: What's that you are saying?

Mrs. Kelleher: A while drunk, a while in fury, tearing the strings and going mad! (*Giving him a nudge.*) And a son that is a gambler. (*Owen starts, but she nudges him.*) Two hands scattering, and but one saving. They spent all we had. There is nothing for you to find in the house, I tell you. It's hard to start a hare out of an empty bush!

Second Williamite: (*Taking sack off bottles.*) Here is something that looks better than holy water. (*Takes up bottle and uncorks it.*)

First Williamite: (*Opening cupboard.*) I see the scut of a hare in this bush!

(*Takes out meat.*)

Second Williamite: (*Drinking.*) Faith, you have a strong cellar. (*Hands on bottle and opens another.*) Here, inn-keeper, have a glass of your own still—drink now to the King.

Matt: I will not. I will not touch one drop from those bottles that are for——

Second Williamite Drink, man; drink till you are in better humour.

Matt: (*Taking glass.*) Well, if I do, I call all to witness that I was forced to it! Four against one, and forced! (*Drinks and holds glass out again.*) And anyway, if I do (*Drinks*), it's not to your master I am drinking, but to King James!

First Williamite: Little I care!   I'd drink to any of them myself, if I had no other way to get it.   Dutch or Scotch, there's no great difference.   If we had a King of our own, that would be another story.

Second Williamite: You have taken your job under William.

First Williamite: And am n't I doing the job, drinking the wine of a Jacobite?   To fight for William by day, and to drink King James's wine by night, is n't that doing double service?

Owen: (*To Mrs. Kelleher.*)   I will go and turn back those that were coming.

Mrs. Kelleher: Do, and God be with you.
(*He goes to door.*)

First Williamite: Stop here, youngster, and drink to the King.

Owen: I will not.

First Williamite: Well, stop and drink against the King.

Owen: I must go.   (*Puts hand on latch.*)

First Williamite: (*Holding him.*)   You have nothing to do that is so easy as this.

Owen: I have colts that are astray to put back on the right road.

First Williamite: A fine lad like you to be running after colts, and King William wanting soldiers!   Come, join our troop, and we'll make a corporal of you.

Owen: Leave me alone. I have my own business to mind.

Second Williamite: The drill would take that stoop out of your shoulders.

First Williamite: It would, and straighten his back. Wait till I drill you! I 'll give you your first lesson. I 'll have you as straight as a thistle before morning. See here now: left, right; left, right; right about face. (*He holds him while the other swings him round.*)

Second Williamite: Give him the balance-step first. Now, youngster, balance step without gaining ground. (*Crooks up Owen's leg.*) See now, this way; stand straight or you will fall over like a sack of potatoes. I should get promotion now; I am training recruits for King William.

Matt: (*Who is by the window.*) Let him go, let him go. There are some persons coming. I hear them. Who now would be coming here so late as midnight?

Second Williamite: Are these our men?

First Williamite: They are not. Our men will be riding.

Owen: (*Passionately.*) Let me go.

Second Williamite: You are not through your drill yet. Here now—(*A knocking at the door.*)

Matt: Customers, maybe. Wait till I open the door.

Owen: (*To Mrs. Kelleher.*)   Don't let him open it!

Mrs. Kelleher: (*Seizing him.*)   Leave opening the door, Matt Kelleher!

Matt: Let me alone! I will open it. It 's my business to open the door.

(*He breaks from her.*)

Mrs. Kelleher: Stop, I tell you! What are you doing? (*Whispers.*)   Don't you know that it might be King James.

Matt: King James! The King outside in the night and we not opening the door! Leave the doorway clear! A welcome, a great welcome to King James!

(*Williamites start up and seize muskets. Kelleher flings the door open. James comes in, followed by Carter and Sarsfield.*)

Owen: (*Shouting.*)   Are you come, strangers, to join King William's men?

First Williamite: They are wearing the white cockade!

Second Williamite: They belong to James, sure enough.

Matt: (*Seizing James's hand.*)   My thousand welcomes to you! And tell me, now, which of you is King James?

James: (*Going back a step.*)   This is a trap!

Carter: Not a doubt of it!

First Williamite: Fire, fire quick! Bring back our troop!

> (*They raise their muskets. Sarsfield rushes past James, seizes the muskets which they are raising so that they are pointed at his own body.*)

Sarsfield: Fire! Yes, here I am! Call back your comrades to bury the King!

Matt: Shame! Shame! Would you kill the King?

First Williamite: We have orders to take him, alive or dead.

Sarsfield: Back, back, put down your muskets! Damn you! Are these Dutch manners?

First Williamite: You are our prisoner. We must call our troop.

Sarsfield: (*Pushing them back angrily.*) Dutch manners! I swear I will not go to prison on an empty stomach! Supper, host, supper! Is a man to be sent empty to his death, even if he be a King?

First Williamite: We have orders. We are King William's men.

Sarsfield: Whoever you are, I will sup here to-night. Hurry, host, hurry. What have you there? Here is a follower of mine who is always hungry. (*Pointing at Carter.*) What have you here? Beef—good—and bread.

> (*Williamites go and stand at door with muskets ready.*)

Matt: (*Bewildered.*) I have, indeed—that is, I had. I had all ready. These traitors came—it failed me to get them out.

Mrs. Kelleher: Leave talking. You have done enough of harm for this night. With your wine-muddled wits you have brought your King to his death. (*She puts plates on table.*)

Sarsfield: (*To Carter.*) Give me a chair. Here (*To James*) are my gloves. (*He sits down.*) You may sit there. (*They sit down, James keeping his face in shadow, and muffled in cloak. They begin eating. To Carter.*) You, I know, are ready for your supper.

Carter: Not a doubt of it! (*He eats greedily.*)

Matt: (*Falling on his knees.*) O forgive me, forgive! To betray my King! Oh! oh! oh! It 's the drink that did it.

Sarsfield: That will do. I forgive, I forgive.

Matt: Take my life! O take my life! I to have brought destruction on my King!

Sarsfield: Get up, old fool. Here, ma'am, those bottles.

Matt: (*Getting up.*) I wish I had died of thirst before I had touched a drop, so I do. The curse of drowning be upon drink, I say!

Sarsfield: (*To First Williamite.*) I am in better humour now. War and hunger make rough manners. Were you in the battle? If so, you are brave men.

First Williamite: We were not in that battle. We were at the Lagan.

Sarsfield: There were good fighters there too. I am sorry they were not on our side. I am sorry all the men of Ireland are not on the one side.

First Williamite: It is best to be on the winning side.

Sarsfield: The winning side—which is it? We think we know, but heaven and hell know better. Ups and downs as with this knife (*Balances it on his finger.*)   Ups and downs.   Winning and losing are in the course of nature, and there's no use in crying.

First Williamite: Some one must be the winner.

Sarsfield: Ups and downs, ups and downs; and we know nothing till all is over.   He is surely the winner who gets a great tombstone, a figured monument, cherubs blowing trumpets, angels' tears in marble—or maybe he is the winner who has none of these, who but writes his name in the book of the people.   I would like my name set in clean letters in the book of the people.

Mrs. Kelleher: (*To James.*)   Take another bit of the beef, sir; you are using nothing at all.   You might have hungry days yet.   Make hay while the sun shines.   It isn't every day that Paddy kills a deer!

James: (*In a muffled voice.*) I have eaten enough.

Mrs. Kelleher: It is well you came before these Northerners had all swept. It's a rogue of a cat would find anything after them.

James: (*Impatiently.*) I have had quite enough.

Mrs. Kelleher: Look now, don't be down hearted. Sure you must be sorry for the King being in danger; but things might change. It is they themselves might be dancing the back step yet. There's more music than the pipes. The darkest hour is before the dawn. Every spring morning has a black head. It's a good horse that never stumbles. The help of God is nearer than the door.

James: Let me be. That is enough.

Mrs. Kelleher: (*Turning away.*) I knew he hadn't enough ate. It's the hungry man does be fierce.

Sarsfield: (*To First Williamite.*) I am sorry not to be able to ask you, fellow-soldier, to sit down with us. But I know you would sooner let the bones show through your coat than lower that musket that is pointing at me. ·

First Williamite: I hope you won't take it unkindly, your Majesty. I am but obeying orders.

Sarsfield: You are right; you are very right in not sitting down. Suppose now you were sitting here, and the door unguarded, and the King should make his escape——

First Williamite: Your Majesty would not get very far—we have other men.

Sarsfield: Who knows? There are ups and downs. A King is not as a common man—the moon has risen—there are horses not far off—he might gallop through the night.

First Williamite: He would be overtaken.

Sarsfield: He might gallop—and gallop—and a few friends would know the sound and would join him here and there. He might go on very fast, away from the harbour, past the wood, his men gathering to him as he passed—to Clonmel——

Second Williamite: Clonmel is full of King James's men, sure enough.

Sarsfield: And then, with all that gather to him there, he would go quietly, very quietly, very quickly to the Gap of the Oaks——

Second Williamite: Listen. That is where the convoy stops to-night.

Sarsfield: A little camp—four hundred horses well saddled, two hundred waggons with powder enough to blow up the Rock of Cashel—and in the middle of all, the yolk of the egg—the kernel of the nut—the pip of the orange.

Second Williamite: He knows that, too. He knows King William is making that secret march.

Sarsfield: A shout—the King! Sarsfield—Ireland!—before there is time to pull a trigger, we have carried off the prize—we have him to treat with *inside* the walls of Limerick. We send the Dutchman back to his country. Will you go with him to the mud-banks, comrades, or will you stop in Ireland with your own King?

First Williamite: The King will win yet. I would never believe that he gave the word to run from the Boyne.

Sarsfield: Now, if I were the King——

Matt: Sure you are King yet, for all I did to destroy you, God forgive me!

Sarsfield: That is true—yes, yes. I am a King to-night, even though I may not be one to-morrow.

Owen: (*Who has been listening eagerly.*) It must be a wonderful thing to be a King!

Sarsfield: Wonderful, indeed—if he have the heart of a King—to be the son and grandson and great-grandson of Kings, the chosen and anointed of God. To have that royal blood coming from far off, from some source so high that, like the water of his palace fountain, it keeps breaking, ever breaking away from the common earth, starting up as if to reach the skies. How else would those who are not noble know when they meet it what is royal blood?

First Williamite: I would know in any place that this King has royal blood.

Second Williamite: It is easy to see among these three which of them is King.

Sarsfield: (*Looking at James.*) A wonderful thing! If he have the high power of a King, or if he take the counsel that should be taken by a King. To be a King is to be a lover—a good lover of a beautiful sweetheart.

First Williamite: I suppose he means the country, saying that.

Second Williamite: I am sure he must have a heart for Ireland.

Sarsfield: He goes out so joyous, so high of heart, because it is never possible for him to do any deed for himself alone, but for her as well that is his dear lady. She is in his hands; he keeps them clean for her; it is for her he holds his head high; it is for her he shows courtesy to all, because he would not have rude voices raised about her.

Second Williamite: The Dutchman would not have those thoughts for Ireland.

Mrs. Kelleher: It's not from the wind he got it. Mouth of ivy and heart of holly. That is what you would look for in a King.

Sarsfield: If she is in trouble or under sorrow, this sweetheart who trusts him, that trouble, God forgive him, brings him a sort of joy! To go out,

to call his men, to give out shouts because the
time has come to show what her strong lover can
do for her—to go hungry that she may be fed;
to go tired that her dear feet may tread safely;
to die, it may be, at the last for her with such
glory that the name he leaves with her is better
than any living love, because he has been faithful,
faithful, faithful!

First Williamite: (*Putting down musket.*)   I
give up the Dutchman's pay. This man is the
best.

Second Williamite: He is the best. It is as
good to join him.

Owen: I will follow him by every hard road
and every rough road through the whole world.

Matt: I will never drink another drop till
he has come to his rights! I would sooner
shrivel up like a bunch of seaweed!

Mrs. Kelleher: It is what I was often saying,
the desire of every heart is the rightful King.

First Williamite: We will follow you! We
will send our comrades away when they come,
or we will turn them to you!

Second Williamite: We will fight for you five
times better than ever we fought for the
Dutchman. We will not let so much as a scratch
on one belonging to you—even that lean-jawed
little priest at the end of the table.

(*Points at James.*)

Sarsfield: (*Rising.*) That is right. I knew you were good Irishmen. Now, we must set out for Clonmel.

James: No, no; we cannot go. We must wait for the men from the French ship.

Sarsfield: Write your orders to them. Tell them to come round, and bring us help at Limerick.

James: It would be best to see them.

Sarsfield: No time to lose! This good woman will give the letter safely.

> (*Carter reluctantly gets out pen and paper. James begins to write. The door opens and the old Lady appears.*)

Owen: It is the poor Lady.

Matt: (*To Sarsfield.*) The poor Lady Dereen, your Majesty, that lost all for the Stuarts.

Owen: Come in, Lady, come; the King himself is here, King James.

Lady: The King! And safe! Then God has heard our prayers!

Owen: Come now, Lady; tell your story to the King.   (*Leads her to Sarsfield.*)

Lady: I lost all for Charles. I will get all back from James. Charles was great; James will be greater! See here I have the King's own seal.

Sarsfield: That is the seal indeed. The King will honour it when he comes to his own.

Lady: No more beggary; no more wandering. My white halls again; my kinsmen and my friends!

Sarsfield: (*To James.*)   Have we any token to give this poor distracted lady?

James: Give her a promise.   We have nothing else to part with.

Sarsfield: (*Taking off his ring.*)   Here, Lady; here is a ring.   Take this in pledge that the King will pay you what he owes.

Lady: (*Taking it.*)   Is it the sunrise?   See how it shines!   I knew the lucky sun would rise at last.   I watched in the east for it every morning.

(*She childishly plays with the ring.*)

Matt: Would n't you thank the King now, Lady, for what he is after giving you?

Lady: I had forgotten.   I forgot I was in the Court!   I was dreaming, dreaming of hard, long roads and little houses—little dark houses.   I forgot I was at Whitehall.   I have not been to Whitehall for a long time to kiss the King's hand. (*She gives her stick to Owen, and stands very tall and straight.*)   I know the Court well.   I remember well what to do.   A curtsy to the right to the Queen (*curtsies*); a curtsy to the left to the princesses (*curtsies.*)   Now I kneel to kiss the King's hand.   (*She sweeps her dress back as if it were a train and kneels.   Sarsfield gives her his hand; she puts her lips to it.   She gets up uncertain*

and tottering, and cries out)—You have befooled
me! That is not the King's hand; that is no
Stuart hand; that is a lucky hand—a strong, lucky
hand!

Sarsfield: You have forgotten, Lady. It was
a long time ago.

Lady: That is no Stuart voice! (*Peers at
him.*) That is no Stuart face! Who was it said
the King is here? (*She looks into Carter's face.*)
That is no King's face. (*Takes his hand.*) That
is no royal hand. (*Going to James.*) Let me
look at your face. (*He turns away.*) Let me
look at your hand.

James: Do not touch me! Am I to be pest-
ered by every beggar that comes in?

Lady: (*In a shriek.*) That is the voice! That
is the voice! (*Seizes his hand.*) That is the hand!
I know it—the smooth, white, unlucky Stuart hand!

> (*James starts up angrily. Williamites have
> gone to listen at the door. "Lillibulero"
> is heard sung outside*)—

Dey all in France have taken a swear,
  Lillibulero bullen a la!
Dat dey will have no Protestant heir:
  Lillibulero bullen a la!
  Lero, lero, lero, lillibulero bullen a la!

Though by my shoul de English do prate,
  Lillibulero bullen a la!

De laws on dere side, and Christ knòws what:
  Lillibulero bullen a la!
  Lero, lero, lero, lillibulero bullen a la!

First Williamite: It is the Newry troop!
Owen: (*Bolting door and putting his back to it.*)
They must not see the King!
Second Williamite: It is too late to escape.
We will fight for you.
Matt: (*Going to door and putting his back to it.*)
Believe me I won't let them in this time.
Sarsfield: (*Drawing sword and going before James.*)   We will cut our way through them.
Mrs. Kelleher: (*Pushing back dresser and opening door.*)   It's a poor mouse that wouldn't have two doors to its hole!   (*She pushes James and Carter in.   Sarsfield stands at it.*)   Go in now. When all is quiet, you can get through to the pier.
Voice of Williamite Captain outside: (*With a bang at door.*)   Open! I say!
Matt: (*Rattling at door while he keeps it fast.*)
Sure, I'm doing my best to open it—if I could but meet with the latch.
Voice: Open, open!
Matt: I have an unsteady hand.   I am after taking a little drop of a cordial—
                    (*Another bang at door.*)
  Owen: I'll quench the light!

(Blows out candles. Sarsfield has followed James. Mrs. Kelleher is pushing dresser back to its place. The door is burst open.)

Captain: Who is here?

Matt: Not a one in the world, Captain, but myself and herself, and the son I have, and a few men of King William's army.

First Williamite: We are here, sir, according to orders.

Captain: Strike a light! (*Williamite strikes it and lights candle.*) What is going on here?

First Williamite: We are watching the pier, sir.

Captain: Why are the lights out?

Matt: It was I myself, sir—I will confess all. It was not purposely I did it. I have an unsteady hand; it was to snuff them I was striving.

Captain: Have you any news of King James?

First Williamite: Great news!

Captain: What is that?

First Williamite: He was seen to the east—up in the wood.

Captain: We must follow him at once.

First Williamite: It is said he is going north—on the road to—Wexford!

Curtain

Act III

Scene: The pier at Duncannon the same night. James and Carter talking together.

James: Upon my word, I am as glad to escape from that dark cellar as I was to get into it an hour ago.

Carter: I wonder how long Sarsfield will be away gathering his men.

James: It should take him a little time; but one never knows with him when he may appear. He makes me start up. He has no feeling for repose, for things at their proper time, for the delicate, leisurely life. He frets and goads me. He harries and hustles. I hear him now! (*Starts.*)

Carter: It is only the French sailors taking away another barrel of their meat from the cellar.

(*French sailors enter from left, singing as before. They roll a barrel away to right.*)

James: The long and the short of it is, it will not be my fault if I spend another night in this abominable island.

Carter: That is good news indeed.

James: The only difficulty is how to get away.

Carter: Why, your Majesty has but to get into the ship.

James: Ah, if I could once get into it! But the question is how am I to escape — from Sarsfield? Of course he is under my orders. I made him obey orders when we left the Boyne. But since then there is something about him — some danger in his eye, or in the toss of his head. Of course, I am in no way afraid of him.

Carter: Of course not, indeed.

James: But for all that, when he begins drawing maps with a flourish of his sword (*Mimics Sarsfield*), or talking as if he were giving out the Holy Scriptures, there is something — a something — that takes away my strength, that leaves me bustled, marrowless, uncertain.

Carter: Not a doubt of it.

James: I am resolved I will strike a blow for myself. I will take my own way. I will be King again. I will be my own master! I am determined that here, this moment, before he has time to come back, before I cool, before my blood goes down, I will make these sailors take me into their boat and row me out to the ship.

Carter: Well said, indeed.

James: When Sarsfield comes back to this pier, if he wants to preach to me again, he will have to swim for it!

Carter: Ha, ha, very good!

> (*Enter sailors from right.*)

James: (*To sailors.*)   Here, my men.   I must go to the ship at once.   You must take me in your boat.

First sailor: Boat not ready yet, sir.   More meat, more pork, more sau-sa-ges.

James: I must go at once.   Here, I will give you money if you will take me at once.

Sailor: Give it now, sir, and I will take you (*James gives it*)—after one more barrel.

James: At once!

Sailor: At once, sir.   Only *one* more barrel.   I will not be two, three minutes.   You go, sir, wait in the boat.   We will follow you very quick.

> (*They go left.*)

James: Come to the boat at once, Carter.   We shall be safe there.   Oh, once at sea I shall be King again!

Carter: Not a doubt of it!

James: Come, come, no time to lose!

> (*They turn right. Music is heard from right, "Lillibulero" suddenly turning into "White Cockade." The two Williamites appear playing fife and drum, Owen with them.*)

First Williamite: That is right!   We are changing the tune well now.   We had to keep up the old one so long as our Newry comrades

were within hearing. That they may have a quick journey to Wexford!   Now for the white cockade!
> (*Owen gives them each one, and they put them in their hats.*)

Owen: You did well, getting leave to come back and to watch the pier.

Second Williamite: So we will watch it well

James: Let me pass if you please.

First Williamite: Where are you going, my little priest?

James: I am going on my own business. Let me pass.

First Williamite: I don't know about that. I have orders to watch the pier. Double orders. Orders from King William to let no one leave it, and orders to let no one come near it, from King James.

James: I tell you I am going on King James's business.

First Williamite: He will be here in a minute. He is gathering men and horses below to the west of the town.   Wait till he comes.

James: No, no, I cannot wait. (*Tries to get through.*)

First Williamite: You will have to wait. No hurry! The Mass can't begin without you!

James: I can make you let me go with one word.

Second Williamite: (*Catching hold of him.*)

Faith, I can hold you without any word at all.

James: (*Wrenching himself free.*) Back, fool, back. I am the King!

Both the Williamites: Ha, ha, ha! Ho, ho, ho!

Second Williamite: O the liar!

Carter: You must believe His Majesty.

First Williamite: I do, as much as I believe you yourself to be Patrick Sarsfield.

Owen: *That* Patrick Sarsfield!

Carter: How dare you doubt that this is the King?

First Williamite: I don't. I have no doubt at all upon the matter. I wouldn't believe it from Moses on the mountain.

James: You common people cannot re-cognise high blood. I say I am the King. You would know it quickly enough if you could see me in my right place!

First Williamite: We might. Your reverence would look well upon the throne. Here, boys, make a throne for His Majesty. (*They cross hands and put him up as if on a throne.*) Hur-rah! This is the third King we have shouted for within the last six hours!

James: Let me down, I say!

First Williamite: Throw out gold and silver to the crowd! Every King throws out gold and silver when he comes to the throne!

Second Williamite: Give us our fee! Give us an estate! I would like mine in the County Meath.

First Williamite: Can you touch for the evil? Here is a boy that has the evil! We'll know you are a King if you can cure the evil!

All: Ha, ha, ha! Ho, ho, ho!

James: Let me down, traitors!

(*A sound of keening heard.*)

Owen: Here is the poor Lady.

(*She comes in keening. They put down the King.*)

James: Here is a witness for me. She knew me last night.

Carter: She knew the true King's hand.

James: Lady Dereen, you knew me last night. Tell these fools what they will not believe from me, that I am the King.

(*She begins keening again.*)

James: (*Touching her arm.*) Look at me. Am I not a Stuart? Touch my hand. Am I not the King?

(*He holds out his hand; she takes it, looks vacantly at it, drops it, and is silent for a minute.*)

Lady: (*Crying out.*) The King! There is no King! The King is dead; he died in the night! Did you not hear me keening him? My lord is dead, and my kinsmen are dead, and my heart is dead; and now my King is dead! He gave his father a bad burying; we will give him a good burying—deep, deep, deep. Dig under the rivers, put the mountains over him; he will never rise again. He is dead, he is dead! (*She sits down rocking herself and sings.*)

Ochone, ochone, my pleasant Stuart;
Ochone, heart-secret of the Gael!

(*Sarsfield comes in hurriedly, motions them all back. Speaks to James.*)
Sarsfield: All is well, sir. Our men are coming in fast. There are two hundred of them to the west of the harbour. We are late for the surprise—that chance is gone; but we can bring good help to hearten Limerick. The King's presence will bring out the white cockade like rush-cotton over the bogs.

James: Yes, yes; very good, very good.

Sarsfield: Are you ready, sir?

James: Oh, yes, ready, very ready—to ⌐leave this place.

Sarsfield: This way, sir, this way!

James: I know the way; but I have left my papers—papers of importance—in that cellar. I must go back and get them.

Sarsfield: Now William's troop has left, I

will have the horses brought to the very edge of the pier—all is safe now.

James: Yes, yes, I am sure there is no danger. Yes, go for the horses; take care they are well saddled.

> (*He goes out left; Sarsfield right. Matt and Mrs. Kelleher come on from left.*)

Mrs. Kelleher: And is it true, Owen, my son, that you are going following after the King?

Owen: It is true, surely.

Mrs. Kelleher: You that would never stir from the hearth to be taking to such hardship! Well, I would n't like to be begrudging you to the King's service. What goes out at the ebb comes in on the flood. It might be for profit.

Matt: Here is the belt your grandfather owned, and he fighting at Ross; pistols there are in it. Do your best now for the King. I 'll drink —no, I swore I would never drink another drop till such time——

Mrs. Kelleher: There is my own good cloak for you—there is something in the pocket you will find no load. (*Owen puts on cloak and belt.*) And here 's cakes for the journey—faith, you 'll be as proud now as a cat with a straddle!

Owen: You will hear no story of me but a story you would like to be listening to. Believe me, I will fight well for the King.

> (*Sailors come from left, rolling a very large*

*barrel; they are singing their song.
Carter is walking after it.)*

Matt: Stop there! What is that barrel you
are bringing away?

Sailor: It is one bacon-barrel.

Matt: It is not. It is one of my big wine
barrels.

Sailor: Oh, ah! I assure you there is meat in it.

Matt: (*Putting his hand on it.*) Do you
think I would not know the size of one of my
own barrels if I met with it rolling through the
stars? That is a barrel that came from France,
and it full of wine.

Carter: (*To sailors.*) Go on with the barrel.

Matt: I will not let it go! Why would I let
my good wine go out of the country, even if I can
have no more than the smell of it myself? Bring
it back to the cellar, I say, and go get your
meat.

Carter: It must be taken to the ship. It is
the King's wish.

Matt: The King's wish? If that is so—where
is the King, till I ask him?   (*Looks around.*)

Carter: I tell you it must go. I will pay
you for it—here is the money. What is its worth?

Matt: Well, if you pay fair, I have nothing to
say. If it was to the King himself it was going,
I would take nothing at all. He would be
welcome.

Carter: (*Giving money.*)   Here, here.   (*To sailors.*)   Go on, now; hurry!   Be careful!

First Williamite: It is a pity now, to see good wine leaving the country, and a great drouth on the King's good soldiers.

Second Williamite: He should not begrudge us a glass, indeed.   It will strengthen us for all we will have to do at Limerick.   (*Puts his hand on barrel.*)

Carter: This belongs to me!   This is my property.   If you commit robbery, you must account to the King!

Matt: Look here, I have still-whiskey in a jar.   I brought it out to give you a drop to put courage into you before you would go.   That is what will serve you as well.

First Williamite: We will let the barrel go, so.

Second Williamite: We could bring away the jar with us.   I would sooner have wine now to drink the King's health.

Lady: (*Standing up, suddenly, and coming in front of barrel.*)   Wine, wine, for the King's wake!

Second Williamite: Listen to her!   That is a good thought.   We will drink to the King living, and she will drink to him dead.

Lady: (*To Matt.*)   Wine, wine, red wine! Do you grudge it for the King's wake?   White candles shining in the skies, red wine for the King's pall-bearers!

(She lifts up her hands.)

First Williamite: She is right, she is right. *(To Matt.)* Since you yourself turned sober, you are begrudging wine for the King! Here!

(Tilts up barrel. A muffled groan is heard from inside.)

Second Williamite: That is a queer sort of a gurgling the French wine has—there is ferment in it yet. Give me an awl till I make a hole.

(Another stifled groan.)

Carter: Oh, oh, oh, oh!

(Puts his cloak over his ears, and retires to back.)

First Williamite: *(Taking out bayonet.)* Here, let me at it!

(Knocks head off barrel; Carter giving short groans at every stroke.)

Carter: Oh! be gentle.

First Williamite: Never fear. I have no mind to spill it. *(Takes off top.)*

(The King stands up, pale and shaking. His cloak has fallen off, and chain and Order are displayed.)

First Williamite: It is the little priest!

Second Williamite: Is he King yet? Or fairy?

Matt: *(Looking in.)* Would any one, now, believe that he has drunk the barrel dry!

First Williamite: I wish I had been in his place.

Mrs. Kelleher: It is trying to desert he was. That 's as clear as a whistle.

Owen: The traitor! Wanting to desert the King!

Matt: But will any one tell me now, what in the wide world did he do with all the wine?

Lady: Is not that a very strange coffin, a very strange coffin to have put about a King?

Mrs. Kelleher: Here is King James!

(*They all turn to right. Sarsfield comes in. He stands still.*)

Owen: Deserting your Majesty, he was!

Matt: Making away in my barrel!

First Williamite: Having drunk all the wine!

Mrs. Kelleher: Let a goat cross the threshold, and he 'll make for the altar!

Sarsfield: (*Taking off his hat.*) Your Majesty!

James: I wish, General Sarsfield, you would control this dangerous rabble

All: Sarsfield!

Mrs. Kelleher: Who are you at all?

Sarsfield: I am Patrick Sarsfield, a poor soldier of King James.

Mrs. Kelleher: And where, in the name of mercy, is King James?

Sarsfield: You are in His Majesty's presence.

(*He goes to help James out of barrel.*)

All together: *That* His Majesty!

Mrs. Kelleher: It seems to me we have a wisp in place of a broom.

Owen: Misfortune on the fools that helped him!

First Williamite: Is it for him we gave up William?

Matt: And that I myself gave up drink!

Sarsfield: (*Who has helped the King out of the barrel, takes him by the hand.*) Any roughness that was done to the King was done, I am sure, unknowingly. But now, if there are any little whisperings, any hidden twitterings, as to what His Majesty has thought fit to do, it is I myself who will give a large answer! (*He unsheaths sword.*)

James: I have business in France. You may stay here, General Sarsfield, if you will. But I will lead you no longer; I will fight no more for these cowardly Irish. You must shift for yourselves; I will shift for myself.

Carter: Not a doubt of it!

James: (*Going off, stops and turns.*) When I come back as a conqueror, with my armies and my judges, there are some I may pardon—my servants who deserted me, my daughters who turned against me. But there are some I will never forgive, some I will remember now and ever, now and for ever—those of you who

stopped the barrel, those who tilted it up, and
those who opened it!

> (*He goes out right followed by Sarsfield
> and sailors. Owen, throwing off cloak
> and belt, and tearing cockade from
> his hat, throws himself down and begins
> to play jackstones as in First Act.*)

Lady: (*Turning to face the other way.*)   Where
is the sun? I am tired of looking for it in
the east. The sun is tired of rising in the east;
it may be in the west it will rise to-morrow!

Mrs. Kelleher: Gone is he? My joy be with
him, and glass legs under him! Well, an empty
house is better than a bad tenant. It might be
for profit.

Matt: (*Taking up jar.*) Well, I am free from
my pledge, as the King says, now and ever, now
and for ever! (*Drinks from jar.*) No more
pledges! It 's as well to be free. (*He sits down
beside Owen.*)

First Williamite: Which King are we best
with; the one we left or the one that left us?

Second Williamite: Little I care. Toss for it.
(*Tosses a penny.*) Heads, William; harps, James!

First Williamite: (*Picking it up.*) Heads it is.
(*Taking cockade from his hat.*) There 's good-bye
to the white cockade.

> (*He and the others throw cockades on the
> ground, and walk off.*)

Mrs. Kelleher: (*To Owen.*)   And what will you
be doing, Owen?   You will hardly go fighting
now.

Owen: What business would I have fighting?
I have done with kings and makings of kings.
(*Throws up jackstones and catches all.*)   Good,
that's buttermilk!

Mrs. Kelleher: You are right; you are right.
It's bad changing horses in the middle of a ford.
(*She takes back her cloak.*)   Is all safe in the
pocket?   It's long before I'll part with it again—
once bit, twice shy.   It might all be for profit.

> (*Sarsfield comes back.   Stands still a minute,*
> *holding hat in his hand.   Lets sword*
> *drop on the ground.*)

Sarsfield: Gone, gone; he is gone—he betrayed
me—he called me from the battle—he lost me
my great name—he betrayed Ireland.   Who is
he?   What is he?   A King or what?   (*He pulls
feathers one by one from cockade.*)   King or knave
—soldier—sailor—tinker — tailor — beggarman—
thief!   (*Pulls out last feather.*)   Thief, that is it,
—thief.   He has stolen away; he has stolen our
good name; he has stolen our faith; he has stolen
the pin that held loyalty to royalty!   A thief, a
fox—a fox of trickery!   (*He sits down trembling.*)

Mrs. Kelleher: (*Coming to him.*)   So you have
thrown away the white cockade, Sarsfield, the
same as Owen.

Sarsfield: (*Bewildered.*) The same as Owen?

Mrs. Kelleher: Owen threw away the King's cockade the same as yourself.

Sarsfield: Threw it away! What have I thrown away? Have I thrown away the white cockade?

Mrs. Kelleher: You did, and scattered it
(*Sarsfield lifts his hat and looks at it.*)

Mrs. Kelleher: If you want another, they are here on the ground as plenty as blackberries in harvest.   (*Takes up a cockade.*)

Sarsfield: Give it here to me. (*He begins putting it in his hat, his hand still trembling.*)

Matt: You will go no more fighting for King James! You are free of your pledge! We are all free of our pledge!

Sarsfield: Where is my sword?
(*Mrs. Kelleher gives it. He puts it in sheath.*)

Mrs. Kelleher: Look, now, the skin is nearer than the shirt. One bit of a rabbit is worth two of a cat. It's no use to go looking for wool on a goat. It's best for you fight from this out for your own hand and for Ireland. Why would you go spending yourself for the like of *that* of a king?

Sarsfield: (*Buckling on his sword-belt.*) Why, why? Who can say? What is holding me? Habit, custom. What is it the priests say?— the cloud of witnesses. Maybe the call of some old angry father of mine, that fought two thousand years ago for a bad master! (*He stands up.*) Well, good-bye, good-bye. (*To Mrs. Kelleher, who is holding out cakes.*) Yes, I will take these cakes. (*Takes them.*) It is likely I will find empty plates in Limerick.   (*Goes off.*)

Lady: (*To Mrs. Kelleher.*) Is not that a very foolish man to go on fighting for a dead king?

Mrs. Kelleher: (*Tapping her forehead.*) Indeed, I think there 's rats in the loft!

Lady: (*Tapping her forehead.*) That is it, that is it—we wise ones know it.   Fighting for a dead king!—ha! ha! ha! Poor Patrick Sarsfield is very, very mad!

Curtain

THE DELIVERER

THIS ALSO IS FOR YOU JOHN QUINN

PERSONS
  Ard
  Dan
  Malachi
  Ard's Wife
  Dan's Wife
  Malachi's Wife
  The King's Nurseling
  A Steward
  An Officer
  One or More Soldiers

*Scene: Steps of a palace at the Inver of the Nile.
At bottom of steps Ard, Dan, and Malachi are
mixing mortar and carrying stones. Music
and laughter heard from window of palace
above. Banners with Pharaoh's ensigns, hawk,
globe, and sun. The men are in poor clothes
and look tired*

Dan: It is time for the women to be bringing the dinner. I'm near starved with the
hunger.

Ard: Here they are now bringing it. Where
would be the use them coming, and the bell not
to have rung?

> *(Bell rings. They all fling down what is
> in their hands and throw themselves on
> the ground.)*

Malachi: I am racked with raising stones
and bearing them to their place. That is
work I never was reared to.

Dan: What call had our old fathers bringing
us away out of our own place?

Malachi: It was the time of the great hunger

drove them away, the time the palmers on the leaves had the crops entirely destroyed.

Ard: We would be better off there in hungry times itself, than the way we are in this place, with the over-government taking the hens off the floor and the plates from the dresser, and the bed itself from under us with their taxes and with their rates.

Malachi: The time I was rising we were treated fair enough. But the nice stock is all done away with now, and buried and gone to the grave.

Dan: It is a bad story for us they to be wore away.

Malachi: There is nothing left in it at this time but tyrants and schemers.

Dan: We to be back in our own country we could knock a living out of it. It is only an odd time the hunger makes headway. It is often my father told me he had two horses belonging to him, and they drawing loads for eight of his first cousins.

Ard: If it is law it is bad law that keeps us labouring out under the mad sun. A King of Foreign to be getting his own profit through our sweat, and we to be getting poor and getting miserable.

Dan: If we had but the means to shape these boards into some sort of a curragh, and to put pins in it and to settle it with oars like, we might go steer towards our own harbour.

Malachi: You have not the means to do it. Sure at the time of the Flood they were a hundred years making a bark. And if it took but three ships or four to bring the twelve families to this place, three times three would hardly be enough to hold us at this time, and every third man or so bringing a wife along with him.

Dan: There is a troop of ships out in the Inver at this time, and scraping against the quay. Speckled sails they were putting up and pulling down a while ago.

Ard: It is the King's heir is after being put in command of those ships, and he being come to sensible years. There is talk of a young queen is looking out from her window for him, in Spain or Armenia or some place of the sort. I was picking news out of a man of the Egyptians a while ago. It is more than *that* he was telling me. (*The women come in.*)

Dan: What is it you have for me, astore, within in the fold of your shawl?

Dan's Wife: It is but a bit of cold stirabout.

Dan: It is made but of yellow meal. I'm in dread I might heave it up again. You would n't have e'er a drop of milk?

Dan's Wife: I thought to make kitchen with an eel I chanced in the mud of the river, and I filling a tin can at the brink. But there came a cat of the King's cats into the house, and snapped it off of the plate. I was afeard to lay a hand on him, and he coming from the place he did.

Malachi: You did well to lay no hand on him. Those cats are a class in themselves. To claw you they would, and bite you, and put poison in your veins the same as a serpent, as maybe they might be in the early time of the world.

Malachi's Wife: That 's right. I 'd sooner the mice to be running in and out like chickens than to bring one of them in on the floor.

Ard: To gather here at the steps at the fall of night they do, and to fight and to bawl for the bits are thrown from the King's house.

Ard's Wife: To come into my own little street a one of them did, and left me with nothing but one bare duck.

Ard: It is made too much of they are entirely. One of them to die at any time, to cry and to keen him the owners will, the same as they would a child or a human.

Dan: To meet with one of them in the moonlight I did a while ago. I am not the better of it yet. It went into some sort of a hump, and said it had to walk its seven acres.

I give you my word you would say it to be as big as an elephant.

Ard's Wife: I would n't doubt it, and all they get thrown out from that kitchen. Sure the rinsings of the plates in the servants' hall would grease cabbage for the whole province. Every day is Christmas in that house.

Ard: There is a grand supper to be in it now that the King is come, and his big men and his friends.

Malachi's Wife: Sure the world knows that. It is likely it will be a feast will last through a year and a day.

Ard: It will not but till to-morrow sometime, when the King's nurseling will make his start in the ships.

Ard's Wife: A hundred cooks that are in it, boiling and roasting and mixing cakes, with currants and with caraway seeds. Sure the bacon they have dressed in frying pans, you would smell it through the seven parishes.

Dan: And ourselves dragging with hunger. Nothing to eat or to fall back on.

Ard's Wife: It is the poor know all the troubles of the world.

Malachi: To be a stranger and an exile, that is the worst thing at all. The feet bending under me, and no one belonging to me but God.

Ard: If it is law it is wrong law some to get

their seven times enough, and ourselves never to get our half enough.

Dan: We to be without a peck hardly upon our bones, and that King to be nourished with sweets and fooleries, and his stomach as big as that you would n't know what to make of it.

Malachi: They would not leave us on the face of the earth if it was n't that we do their heavy work.

Dan: Is there another crumb of meal in the handkerchief?

Dan's Wife: There is not, and no earthly thing in the house itself, unless it might be a few young nettles I put down to boil in the pot.

Dan: An ass that would go forage on the highway would get better provision, or the dogs that go preying for themselves.

Malachi's Wife: There is no nature in them at all.

Ard: It is not right and it is not justice, riches to be coming in to them, and they asleep in the bed.

Malachi: I would ask no riches at all besides being in a little village of houses among my own people, that would have a wish for my bones.

Dan: That I may never sin, but I am getting a smell I never felt since my grandfather's time, the smell of a roasted goose!

Ard: It is a smell of wine I am getting, that is giving me a twist-like in the heart.

Malachi's Wife: You would know there to be wine in it, and the laughing is among them, and the stir.

Ard's Wife: There is one of them facing the window—throw your eye on him now—a holy circus for grandeur he is, and having a gold chain about his neck.

Dan's Wife: He is very comely surely and gay. A lovely dotey young man.

Ard: It is easy be comely and be light-hearted, and want or trouble not to have ever come anear you.

Malachi's Wife: Who is he now? Is it he himself is the King's son?

Dan's Wife: He should be that, and he so well-shaped, and curls on every side of his poll, the same as a ridge of peas.

Dan: Sure they all do have curls of that sort in the King's house. I am told it is hair grew on horses' necks, or maybe on the head of a corp. To shape it into rings-like they do, with a bar-like would be reddened in among the coals.

Malachi's Wife: There is not a tailor or a dressmaker in the district slept a wink these seven nights, and all the grand suits were ordered for this big day.

Dan's Wife: There is no one can become his

suit better than that King's son with the laugh
on his mouth.   He should make joy for his lady
of a mother, and she to be looking on him this
day.

Dan: You think yourself very wise now, to be
giving out judgments about kings' sons.

Dan's Wife: Has n't he the lovely face?   His
head held up so lofty and so high, and he having
a hurl in his hand, and a crown of posies on his
brow.

Malachi's Wife: The world has flowed upon
him.   There are some are born having luck
through the stars and through the strength of the
moon.

Dan's Wife: Why would n't he have luck, and
he to be born in the King's own palace?

Ard: That is what he would wish you to be
thinking.

Dan's Wife: Why would n't we think it?   He 's
as nice as you 'd ask.   I see no flaw in him at
all.

Ard: You are thinking him to be far above
myself I suppose?

Ard's Wife: Sure there must be some difference
in station and in blood.   It was the Almighty
Himself put that in the world.

Ard: What would you say hearing he is not
far in blood from ourselves?

Dan: That is what we are after being told,

whether or no it is true. Of our own race and of our tribe.

Malachi: To one of the twelve families he belongs. To the one breed with myself, but that the generations are scattered.

Ard: I heard that, and that his fatner gave in to the hardship.

Malachi: He did so. In heaven he is now, and on earth he was driving cattle.

Dan: And his mother a girl of the Kohaths, threw him out from her on the rising flood.

Malachi: The King's daughter that took notice of him in the flag-flowers, and she washing herself at the time the flood began to slacken down.

Ard: To rear him up as her own she did, and on her death-bed she willed him her father's heir.

Dan: It is on this day he is to be put beyond all the rest nearly of Pharaoh's people.

Malachi: The curse of his own people be on him, he to be frolicking where he is, and treading the stones were quarried through our labour.

Ard : Going here and forth, spending what would buy an estate, sparkling abroad in the fields. Following foxes with huntsmen and hounds, or fowling after snipe and teal. That the whole of them may turn against him, and put their beaks through his guts, or their claws

or whatever disagreeable weapon-like the Lord
may have given them for their own protection
and their aid!

(*Bell heard ringing.*)

Dan: Mind yourselves, boys, there is the
boss at the bell.

Ard: It is his own bones I would wish to
see leaping and swinging up there in the place
the bell is!

Dan: Where's the use talking.   (*Sings.*)

> Trouble I ne'er did find
>   Till I joined the work with the cruel Turk
> At the Inver of the Nile.

Ard: Let ye all draw to silence.   It is the
Nutcrackers is in it.   He is the worst tyrant of
them all.

Dan: He would n't as much as give leave to
rise your back or look around you.   There would
be no labourer alone with him, but would be in
dread he would kill him.

Malachi: That's the way with those low quality
stewards that belong to the middling class.

Ard: The dirty savage!   He'd think no more
of a person's life than he would of a crow.

Dan: Whist your tongue.   I would say he
has drink taken.   It is out of the parlour he is
come.

Steward: (*Coming rather unsteadily down steps.*)
Get back now to your work, you scheming michers!
Bring over mortar there, it is wanting beyond.
These steps had a right to be readied and finished
before the King coming here at all. Go bring
mortar, I say.

Dan: We will, your honour, the very minute
it will be ready.

Steward: It should be ready by this, and you
not to be sleeping and idle and playing odd and
even with bits of stones.

Malachi: It failed us to mix it, the lime being
all used and spent.

Steward: How well you did n't go look for more,
you crippled jackass.

Dan: Sure we went seeking it, and there was
no lime in it, and no stones broken, and no
fire kindled in the kilns.

Malachi: The men had charge of them were
brought away to be blowing the bellows for the
ovens were put up for the King's big dinner.

Steward: It is too much gab you have! It
is well able you are to make up stories and lies.
If it was beef and cabbage you were sent seeking, you would track it out swift enough!

Malachi: We are telling no lies. There is
no lime to be got.

Steward: Let ye mix the mortar, so, without
lime.

Malachi: There is no one, tradesman or college bred man, could mix it without lime.

(*King's Nurseling appears at top of steps and stands behind a pillar.*)

Steward: Let you do it so with your enchantments. You that have the name of being an old prophecy, let you rise up and make it from that bit of a board. Sure, you are able to change yourself into an eel, the same as the King's Druids.

Malachi: There is no reason in what you are saying.

Steward: No, but let you change yourself and your two comrades into the shape of three hares till I 'll go coursing. I 'll engage I 'll come up with you! I 'll put my teeth in you! (*Cracks whip.*) If you can't do no other thing you can make sport for us!

Malachi: Any work I have to do, I will do it fair and honest. There is no justice asking me to do more than that.

Steward: I 'll show you justice! All the justice you have to look for in this place is in my own cat-o'-nine-tails! (*Cracks it.*)

Malachi: Is it to strike me with your lash you would?

Steward: It is, and to strip the hide off of you, to make tacklings will yoke your brood and your litter to the plough. (*Lifts whip.*)

Dan: Ah, now your honour, you will not lay

the whip on Malachi! Old he is and failing from the world. He is delicate, he cannot stand.

Ard: He is no way deserving of cruelty. An honester man never followed a beast. There is not the weight of that on his character.

Steward: There will be the weight of this upon his back!   (*Flourishes whip.*)

Malachi: Take care but I will stop your hand!

Steward: Is it to your devils you are calling now, and to the witches of the air? It is not to flog you I will be satisfied. You 'll be making provision for the crows to-night if there 's a rope to be found in Egypt!

Malachi: I will call for help to the King's nurseling. Let him say am I to be abused.

Steward: The King's nurseling! Ha, ha, ha! Is it that you are thinking that one will come to your help?

Malachi: It is certain he would be able to save a man from the foot of the gallows.

Steward: Is it the like of ye he would stretch out to, and the whole shoal of ye to be dying like fish? Did n't you hear the trumpets braying for him since morning? This is his big day. Sure, myself and the rest of the bailiffs and the stewards are after drinking to his good health!

Malachi: He is of our race.

Steward: If he was n't you might have some chance. He 'd as soon confess himself to be a

pig of a herd of pigs. He that was reared to
the army, and is apt to be made king in the
finish.

Malachi: We are as good as him, but that we
are drowned under trouble.

Steward: Ye are, and under dirt and filth.
He would n't come anear you or within three
perches of you unless it might be to be picking
fun out of you. Ye that use neither head bath
or body bath.

Malachi: There was one of his family joined
with my own family in marriage, two hundred
years ago.

Steward: You to say that in his hearing,
he'd knock the wits out of you, as quick as
the blast of a pipe.

Malachi: I tell you it is as true as that God's
sunlight is shining upon us.

Steward: So it is, and as true as that there's
a tail on Pharaoh's cat. Why would n't it
be true, and he the very dead spit and modelling
of yourselves? He should know that every time
he would look in a body glass. (*King's Nurseling moves as if startled.*) But to let on that
it is true, he'd sooner drown himself on the
race course, that is at this time under flood.

Malachi: He to know the whole truth he will
help us.

Steward: He will not. Very high up in

himself ‿he is.　He would think you to be no
credit to him.　Very proud and stiff;—and if it
was n't for the King's kindness, and the King's
daughter that picked him from the gutter, it is
squealing under the lash he would be at this
minute the same as yourselves.　The King's
nurseling!　A scamp that is ignorant of his mother
and of his father along with that!

King's Nurseling: (*Coming before them suddenly.*)　What are you saying?

Steward:　Oh, sir, your honour, I said nothing,
nothing at all worth while!

King's Nurseling:　I heard what you said.

Steward:　Sure, you never thought it was of
your honour I was speaking.　I would never do a
thing like that.　I was talking of—of a mermaid's
son my grandmother used to be telling me about,
and she enticing me to stop beside the hearth.

King's Nurseling:　You said I was one of
these common men.

Steward:　Oh, sir, what are you saying?
What trade or what consanguinity could there
be between the like of you that was reared in
golden cradles, and these slaves, these paupers,
these tricksters, rebels, liars, herds, sheepstealers,
worms of the earth, rogues of the highway,
thieves, informers?

Malachi:　Stop your lies!　We had some in
our generations that never knew the power of

death. We had saints and angels visiting our old fathers, before ever there was a Pharaoh on the Nile!

Steward: Listen, sir, to that! That's rebellion! That's treason-felony! That word will have you hanged! Call out now your soldiers, sir! (*He seizes Malachi and strikes him.*)

King's Nurseling: Leave your hold. (*Strikes Steward with his hurl. He reels and falls back out of sight over the steps.*)

Malachi: He is dead!

Ard: He has his neck broke.

Dan: That was a good blow and no mistake.

Ard: He has him killed with one blow of the hurl.

King's Nurseling: Throw the carrion in a hole of water! (*Dan and Ard bear him away. The women have gone aside.*)

Malachi: You stood up well to him. It took you to tackle him. You behaved well doing that. But I'm in dread it will bring you under trouble. The punishment for murder is death.

King's Nurseling: I am under trouble from this out, surely.

Malachi: It might not be found out, and you going back quick into the King's house.

King's Nurseling: I would have been long out of that house, if I knew it was not from my own mother and father I had a claim to it.

Malachi: Is that the way with you?

King's Nurseling: Yesterday I was son to the King's daughter, and to-day I do not know, east or west, to what tribe or family I belong.

Malachi: Be satisfied. You are a good man's son.

King's Nurseling: And is it to yourselves I belong by my birth? (*Malachi nods.*) The world knows I never knew that!

Malachi: It is not with ourselves you will stop. We are in danger now to be flogged and tortured and hanged.

King's Nurseling: What way could I have an easy mind in it, and my own people being under cruelty and torment? It is along with you I will stop.

Malachi: Take care now, dear. It would be a pity you to die in your young age.

King's Nurseling: They did a great wrong putting a bad name on my mother's race, and rearing myself to shun and to mock at you, thinking myself a better breed.

Ard : (*Who has come back with Dan.*) Is it that you will take our part?

King's Nurseling: I will not eat bread or take my sleep again in that house. I will banish it from me for ever.

Dan: You do not know well what you are doing, and we being a crushed miserable race.

King's Nurseling: It is not to a crushed miserable race I have a mind to belong.

Dan: Stretch out so to help us, and to bring us away out of this.

Ard: Let you strive to put the fear of God on the King, the way he will let us go free.

Dan: You not to be able to ready the road and to make a path before us, it can be done by no other one.

Ard: They have put great cruelty upon us. It is you are the most likely one might get it taken off.

Dan: There is no one but yourself to look to. Every person in this place is very combined against us.

Malachi: It was dreamed to me it was one from the King's house would take in hand our escape.

King's Nurseling: I will do all I can do.

Dan: Do that, and you will get the blessing of the people.

King's Nurseling: I will bring you out from this disgrace.

Malachi: So he will. That is in the prophecy. I saw it in the clouds of heaven of a winter night. He will win in the end, but he will not pass within the mering of the Land of Promise.

King's Nurseling: Come up with me to a place will have no ears. I have my plans to make. I have commands to give you.   I am thinking I see a road.

(Ard and Dan follow him.   Malachi tries to but fails and sits down.)

Malachi: I have no bend in the leg.   I cannot get up the steps.

King's Nurseling: Stop where you are for a while and take your rest while you can.   When this moon will be over and the next moon begun, we will be back in the place our fathers owned. *(Walks up steps.   The women come and kneel on steps blessing him.)*

Ard's Wife: God love you! My thousand blessings on my two knees to you!

Dan's Wife: That the world may wonder at the luck you 'll have!

Malachi's Wife: That my blessing may comfort you, and make you that you 'll never be broken up!

Dan's Wife: May God increase you!

Ard's Wife: The Lord have mercy on every one belonging to you!

Dan's Wife: And on every one ever went from you!

Malachi's Wife: And on yourself at the latter end.

Ard's Wife: The laugh that is in his eye should be sunshine to ripen the barley, and bleach the flax in the field!

Dan's Wife: The kindest man that ever broke the world's bread!

Malachi's Wife: That he may have the bed of heaven whoever will be left out!

(*King's Nurseling, Dan, and Ard have gone off.*)

Malachi: The Lord be praised it is in my own country my bones will be coffined at the last!

Malachi's Wife: There is a hundred years come into your life with that great news.

Dan's Wife: Is that country I wonder as good as what they say?

Malachi: It is good and kind. The best for meadows and for fair water. Everything a farmer would wish to have around his house he will have it.

Ard's Wife: It is estated people we will be that time. Hay and oats in the haggards, a stack upon every small patch.

Malachi's Wife: Sure the vessels will not hold the milk there, it is down on the ground it must fall. There is honey on the tops of the grass.

Malachi: I to be a beggar on the roads there beyond, I would have neither cark nor care. Keening done away with and treachery. It is a blessed place. There will no snakes live in it. They must perish at the touch of its earth. The sea does be full of all sorts of fish.

Dan's Wife: I heard that. Quality fish it would be easy to be eating. The bones of them will

melt away in the fire.   The smiths do be forging
gold the same as iron.

Ard's Wife: The next young son that will be
born to me, it is not as a slave he will be reared.

Malachi's Wife: Here is Dan coming. He will
say are we in a vision or in a dream!

Dan's Wife: What did the King's Nurseling say
to you? Is it in earnest at all he is?

Dan: He is, surely.   He wanted but the wind
of the word. Believe me that one has a good
head for plans!

Malachi: What way at all will he get us out
of this?

Dan: By the miracles of God, and the virtue
of those ships beyond at the quay.

Malachi's Wife: The ships did you say! That
is a great thought. They should be very an-
swerable.

Ard's Wife: What time will we make our start?

Dan: It is on board of those ships the whole
of us are to go to-night.   There are orders sent to
the rest of the twelve families in secret.   Believe
me, there is a good headpiece on that young boy.

Dan's Wife: And is it to our own country they
will bring us?

Dan: To go voyage with his left hand to
the shore the King thinks he will, and his right
hand to the wideness of the sea. He to be out
of the harbour, it is not that way he will go,

but his left hand to be facing the sea. At the flight of night he will be facing towards a safe harbour near the borders of our own country, and that is free from Pharaoh's rule.

Malachi: He will send his armies after us there.

Dan: It is what the youngster was saying, we to be out of his hand, every enemy has any complaint against Pharaoh will be on our own side. Believe me, he is great for plans.

Malachi's Wife: Ah, it is only foolishness. It is impossible to steal away unknown.

Dan: It is far out in the night we will go, the way they will feel no noise. The choice captains at the supper till morning, the guard will not be without every sort of beer and of wine. The lad has the Heads of Police sent watching higher up the river, putting in their mind that the place being deserted there will be wild lads spearing the King's fish. He is sending provision to the ships; food for eating, gold for bestowing, arms for to banish enemies. For every five pounds of meal he is sending twenty pound of lead. Bags and bags of money he has, gold and notes to the world's end. I wish I did n't wipe the mortar from me awhile ago. There might some of the riches have stuck to my feet.

Malachi's Wife: Let us be going from this ugly place. It will seem to be the length of a year till I will set out,

Ard's Wife: Where now is my man? I would wish to put a white shirt on him before we 'd set out, and to round the corners of his head.

Dan: He was sent to forewarn the neighbours to make ready, and to strengthen themselves for the start. To go borrow the makings of a cake he will bid them, and to boil the soup of a hen.

Dan's Wife: I should go ready the children. I should wish them to put on a good appearance going back to their own country. It is well I have a bleach of clothes out drying on the bush.

Ard's Wife: I got the lend of a little skillet-like from a cook of the King's under-cooks. Copper it is. Would it be any harm I wonder to bring it away in my box?

Malachi's Wife: I 'll make no delay and bring no load with me but to put my apron about my head and to walk out of this. Look at what came to me from my father and he dying. The key of the housedoor in my own village. It is here in the bosom of my dress. I have but to turn it going in, and to sit down beside the hearth.

Ard's Wife: It is likely it is a tribe of grabbers you will find on the hearth before you.

Malachi: If there are grabbers there before us we will know a way to make them quit.

Ard's Wife: We 'll be plentiful from this out surely.

Dan's Wife: There 'll be currant cakes on the table next Shrove!

Malachi: No strangers to be meddling with us, and leave to keep the feast days and to gather to prayers.

Dan's Wife: Let you shout out now for the King's whiteheaded boy!

Malachi: He is good and he looks good. He is the best we ever met!

Ard's Wife: As simple as if he wasn't worth a shilling, and he dealing out money in sacks.

Dan's Wife: A real blood he is!

Dan: Ah, he is no great family man. Just a clean family, that's all.

Malachi: A man that ignorance was hid from. He should know the seven languages!

Ard's Wife: We should knock great comfort out of him. He is no way flighty but good.

Dan's Wife: The skin of his face showed out as fair as a sovereign. He has seven colours in his clothes!

Dan: I'm not too bad-looking myself, and I to have good means and a good way and not to be poor and badly clad.

Dan's Wife: The sweet eyes and the smile of him! He is a dear loughy man!

Dan: That is enough of gab about himself and his looks. Let you stop your clatter and your talk!   (*Ard comes in.*)

Ard's Wife: The sea and the hills would go bail for him! Sure that one would have no harm in him no more than a child.

Dan's Wife: We will lift him up on our shoulders passing every bad spot on the road! We'll have a terrible illumination for him the day we will come to our own!

Ard's Wife: We will, and put out shouts for him through the whole of the seven parishes! His name will be more lasting than the cry of the plover on the bog!

Ard: You are very ready to give praises and to give trust to one you never cast an eye on till this day.

Ard's Wife: Sure any one would think more of a stranger than of a person they would know.

Malachi's Wife: We have good dependence on him. He is kind hearted and willing hearted.

Ard's Wife: What could he be but good, and he after making every gap easy before us?

Dan: The women are that cracked after him. You would say they never got a sight of any man besides a cripple or a deformed person before this day.

Ard: That is the way with women and fools. All that is new is beautiful. There'll be another telling by and by.

Malachi's Wife: I would say him to be a nice man and a good man for the world.

Ard: Wait a while till we'll see what way will he turn out. He didn't give us our travelling charges yet.

Dan: I wouldn't begrudge him praise, and I being certain he deserved it.

Ard: He didn't behave too decent not leaving us so much as a red halfpenny to drink his health. What way can we be sure this voyage will not be more for killing than for profit?

Dan: That is true for you. Has he skill to bring us ploughing over the hills and hollows and the rough headed rocks of the sea? The narrow sea or the wide?

Malachi: He to have said he will rise us up out of our trouble, he will do it.

Ard: It would be a pity going so far, and black sails maybe to be put up for us before we would come to land. Well, drowning is laid down to be an easy death.

Ard's Wife: It is often I heard my grandmother saying there are great baulks and great dangers on the road, and a red stream that does be boiling with the heat.

Dan's Wife: It might be he has flying ships— or that the whole of the stream and of the ocean would open before him, he being blessed.

Ard's Wife: The blazing mountain she used to be talking of, and the mountain of needles.

Dan's Wife: It is likely he has enough of a charm

to change the points of the needles to green rushes, and to bring us through the fire shivering.

Ard: I'm in dread it is to put a good mouth on himself he made big promises, and to leave us in worse case after.

Ard's Wife: I am thinking myself it will fail us to make our escape.

Dan's Wife: He to put a sleeping-pin through Pharaoh's plaits, it will keep him in the feathers through the length of nine days and nine nights.

Ard's Wife: Where would be the use, and the King having three times fifty beagles and three hundred soldiers at every cross road and every open road? There could n't so much as a rib of hair go pass athrough them unbeknownst.

Dan's Wife: To put a mist-like about them he might, the way they would go astray and be striking and hitting at one another and at themselves.

Dan: I'm in dread whatever way it is, we will have a queer long road to travel.

Ard: That is true for you. I met with a priest of the King's priests, and I coming out over the threshold of the youngster's office. To stop and to talk with me he did. A very friendly man; and shook hands with me and gave me the hand out.

Dan: Is it that he will help us to make our escape?

Ard: It is likely he made a guess I had some

notion of the sort in my mind. He was bidding me go quiet and easy, and the King would be apt to come around, and to let us go free in the heel.

Malachi: I would have no trade with him or the like of him. The Egyptians, you never can get at the root of them.

Ard: I, now, to draw up a petition, he was saying——

Malachi: You won't get the breadth of the black of your nail that way. They will give us what we will take ourselves, that is what they will do.

Ard: There might be some of themselves would speak for us to the over-Government.

Malachi: Ah, what way would we wrench it out of the Government? To say that we will is only vanity!

Ard: It is what the priest was saying, the lad is proud and he is giddy. He is no way religious, he was saying, on the one or the other side.

Malachi's Wife: It would be a pity surely if he would not be stiff in his religion.

Ard: He to have broke out of their creed, and not to have joined in our own, he would not be a fitting leader for ourselves. According to what I am told, he's a real regular Pagan.

Ard's Wife: I would be sorry to think he

would be ignorant and not able to say off the Catechism.

Malachi: Whatever he might be, we would be better off with him than with them we are under at this time.

Ard: It's hard know. Some are terrible wicked, but some are fair enough.

Malachi: I would make no complaint, getting bad treatment from a person would be natural, and of our own tribe, besides the foreign troop. It is going trafficking with the Egyptians has you sapped and destroyed.

Malachi's Wife: A priest of the Egyptians to be mistrustful of him, it is likely our own priests would not wish us to have dealings with them.

Ard's Wife: You may be certain of that.

Malachi: So you may be too. Hit one and you hit all. That's the way with clergy rule.

Ard: He to be picking knowledge out of ourselves, he might maybe get through all the dangers and into the good country. It is himself would take the credit then, and be maybe craving to make our laws.

Malachi: I was thinking before this it was jealousy rose up in your head, and that gave you a spleen against him.

Ard's Wife: Look at him! Is it himself at all is in it?

(*King's Nurseling walks across at back.
He is wearing poor clothes like their
own.*)

Malachi's Wife: Take care has he the evil eye
put upon us. He gave us no blessing as he
passed.

Ard's Wife: He is no great gaff, and not having the grand clothes that he had, and the
top-knot and the fringes.

Malachi's Wife: He has put on poor clothes
like our own for a mockery.

Dan's Wife: Take care might it be spying on
us he is come.

Ard's Wife: To come as a spy and an informer,
that is a foul thing to do.

Malachi's Wife: I am a very bad lover of
deceit and of treachery.

Dan's Wife: It was a queer story his mother
to go cast him out of her hand, and leave him
to be reared by strangers.

Ard's Wife: Ah, how do we know was she wed
at all at that time?

Malachi's Wife: That he may never come back
alive or dead! I never will give in to a Pagan.
I have promised God and the priest.

Malachi: Is it going against him ye are,
and turning from praising to dispraising and
abuse?

Malachi's Wife: Why would you go taking his

side, and the whole of the rest of us being against him?

Malachi: I was acquainted with his grand-father. It is a bad day I would see him wanting a friend.

Malachi's Wife: You to be peaceable to this frog of the ditches, I will not be peaceable to yourself.

Malachi: I tell you there is no other one can bring us out of this.

Ard: Take care but there might be.

Malachi: There will not be any other one.

Ard: I would not be sure of that. I never heard that lad to have said two words upon a platform.

Malachi: It is easy be handy in talk, and be supple. Is it that you yourself is thinking to free us?

Ard: The ships are ready. We have the password. Anyone could do the job now.

Dan: I'm as great a story as yourself any day. If any one of us is to take the lead, I have a mind to take it myself.

Ard: I won't give in to that, or to you putting out challenges of the sort.

Malachi: Let you leave it to the man at the plough to drive the furrow to the end.

Dan: What I will not do is give Ard scope to be tricking, the way he will put him-

self on top. It 's a mean thing to trick.
I never would be trickish if I was to die with
hunger.

Ard: Is it a man of your sort any person
would take commands from?

Dan: You to be arguing like a consequential! A chap that could n't put a jackdaw
on a farm of land!

Ard: I 'm able to put a name on you, that
you are not more like doing a good deed than
a deed of treachery.

Malachi: Stop your chat! The noise you
are making would bring upon us the whole
army of police.

Dan: Why would I stop? He 'd eat the
head off me, and I 'm not to eat him!

Ard: The latter end of the world to be to-
morrow, I 'd tell him he is not fit so much
as to put fetters on a sheep!

Dan: Have a care now, or I 'll whitewash the
steps with your bones!

Ard: I don't wish you any harm, but God
is unjust if you die a natural death!

Dan: The curse of my heart on you!

Ard: A short course to you!

Dan: You cur, you disgrace, you!

Ard: Keep your tongue off me, you rags!
That bad luck may follow you! You that
are a rogue since the first day you were born!

Malachi: (*Seizing Dan.*) Put the malice out of your heart or we are all destroyed!

Dan: Leave me alone! I am well able to best him!

Ard: You may set your coffin making, for I 'll beat you to the ground!

Dan: It was n't to-day or yesterday I learned to know your tricks!

Dan's Wife: Leave go of one another!

Ard: I will not till I squeeze the breath out of him!

Ard's Wife: Leave your hold!

Malachi's Wife: Let some person drag them asunder!

Dan's Wife: They to get in an argument, it is hard part them from one another!

Ard's Wife: Oh, they are in flows of blood!

Dan: I 've a grip of you now, you mean little tinker!

Ard: I 'll knock the head of you, you shameful pauper!

Dan: Wait till I 'll hit him a kick!

Ard: You common rascal!

Dan: You rap! You vagabone!

All: Oh, let you stop! They 'll kill one another!

> (*King's Nurseling comes out, parts them
> quickly, throws down Ard, holds Dan.*)

King's Nurseling: Are you fools? Damning

and blasting and cursing and shouting and beating one another! You will bring out the whole of the palace!

Ard: I done nothing. He drew a blow at me. I gave him but one box. .

Dan: He did, and a pelt of a stone and a slap of the left hand on the jaw.

King's Nurseling: You are on the brink of your escape! Keep your uproar till you are out of this! (*Shoves down Ard who tries to rise.*)

Ard: Leave knocking me. Have you a minb to make an end of me with a blow of a hurl the same as the Nutcracker a while ago?

Ard's Wife: Let you leave meddling with my man!

Dan's Wife: Take off your hand! It is not in a bunch of rushes my own man was reared!

Malachi's Wife: Take care will he call to the soldiers for to have us all destroyed.

Ard's Wife: We are in great danger that he will. It would be right gag his mouth.

Dan's Wife: It's best make an end of him.

Ard's Wife: It would be no harm to quiet him, giving him a prod of a knife.

Malachi's Wife: A real idolater he is. That is what the King's priest said.

Malachi: Is it at the bidding of the Egyptians you will give up the man of your own race?

Ard: He will betray us to the King's men.

King's Nurseling: I have broken with that troop altogether.

Ard: You will fail us yet, and the King to speak out stiff to you!

King's Nurseling: I tell you he to hinder us, I will redden that tide beyond, and twist a bit of crape on every house-door in Egypt.

Malachi: That is right, that is right! That is the clean drop stirring in him!

Dan's Wife: It is misleading us he is.

Malachi's Wife: A man to do that it would disgust you.

Ard's Wife: That my curse may follow him!

Dan's Wife: That his path may be as slippery as the ditch where he was born, if he did kill the King's steward.

Malachi's Wife: A long trembling to you!

Malachi: They are set on mischief. The very most people he did good to.

King's Nurseling: If you all turn against me, I will fight on with my back to the wall.

Ard: We will give no place to spies!

Dan: We will leave you no time to be an informer!

Malachi: Ye are doing a great wrong! Give him a show and a hearing!

Ard: It's best make an end of him!

Dan: He can lodge no complaint that time!

Malachi: Ye are mad, raging mad!

(*Ard pushes King's Nurseling down on step.*)

Malachi's Wife: (*Throwing a stone.*) Frog spawn!

Ard's Wife: (*Throwing a stone.*) Foundling!

Dan's Wife: (*Throwing a stone.*) By child!

Ard's Wife: (*Throwing a stone.*) Drownded whelp!

(*All throw stones. King's Nurseling sinks back.*)

Officer: (*Appearing from palace, striking gong.*) Where is the King's Nurseling!

(*All shrink back leaving King's Nurseling on step.*)

Officer: (*Loud.*) The pipes and the flutes are ready! The boiled is ready and the roast! (*Sees King's Nurseling.*) Rise up, you drowsy vagabone, and say did you see the King's Nurseling in any place?

King's Nurseling: The King's Nurseling?

Officer: The supper ready and no leave to begin till he will come that is at the head of all. (*Strikes gong.*) I wish I never lost sight of him.

King's Nurseling: He will not go back to the supper. He is facing towards the wilderness of the marsh.

Officer: It is blind drunk you are and little you know about him.

(*Kicks King's Nurseling and goes away*

sounding gong. King's Nurseling's head droops. He sinks back on the ground. The others come back cautiously.)

Ard: There is no one to take notice of us. We can make our escape to the ships.

Dan: (*Looking at King's Nurseling.*) There is no stir in him. I thought the life would not have left him so quick.

Ard: Leave him there where he is.

Dan: Take care would they find him and know his features, and follow after us to get revenge for his death.

(A loud mewing and screaming heard.)

Dan's Wife: What is that screeching?

Malachi's Wife: It is the King's cats calling for their food.

Ard: Shove him over the steps to them.

Malachi: Will you throw him to the King's cats?

Dan's Wife: A good thought. No one will recognise him. They 'll have the face ate off him ere morning.

Ard's Wife: Throw him to the King's cats!

(They screech again. Their shadow is seen on steps. King's Nurseling is dragged into darkness. A louder screech heard.)

Officer: (*Coming back.*) What is this uproar of cats? Or is it the yelping of yourselves that are curs.   It is the whole of this troop that is drunk and howling.   (*Takes up whip and shakes it.*)   Stop your ugly noise!

(*A soldier appears.*)

Officer: Send out a squad of the guard to lodge these bawling blackguards in the black hole.   Here, put on the handcuffs. (*Soldier comes and handcuffs them leaving them crouching on the steps.*)

Officer: Sound out a loud call.   I did n't find him yet.

(*He goes up to door.   A loud blast of trumpets is heard.*)

Malachi: I 'm on the seventy since last July. It is old bones I will leave in the gaol.

Ard: We were never destroyed out and out till now.   It is in bad case we are this time surely.

Dan: It is you yourself was the first to overthrow and to banish him.

Malachi: (*Laughing to himself.*)   They were said to give him learning and it is bad learning they gave him.   That young man to have read history he would not have come to our help.

Malachi's Wife: Well, the story is done now, and let you leave it to God.

Malachi: It is sorrow you will sleep with from this out.   You will not find the like of him from the rising to the setting sun.

Dan's Wife: Look! He is living yet. He is passing!

> (*King's Nurseling passes slowly at foot of steps towards right. His clothes are torn and blood-stained and he walks with difficulty.*)

Dan: It is but his ghost. He is vanished from us.

Dan's Wife: I wish I did n't turn against him. I am thinking he might be an angel.

Dan: (*To Malachi.*) Will he ever come back to us?

Malachi: I won't tell you what I don't know. Wandering, wandering I see, through a score and through two score years. Boggy places will be in it and stony places and splashes—and no man will see the body is put in the grave. A strange thing to get the goal, and the lad of the goal being dead. (*Another screech of the cats. He laughs.*) I would n't wonder at all he to bring back cross money to shoot the cats. He will get satisfaction on the cats.

Curtain

MUSIC FOR THE
SONGS IN THE PLAYS
NOTES AND CASTS

MUSIC FOR THE CANAVANS

MUSIC FOR THE WHITE COCKADE

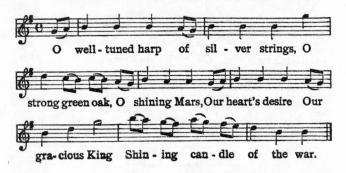

O well - tuned harp of sil - ver strings, O
strong green oak, O shining Mars, Our heart's desire Our
gra - cious King Shin - ing can - dle of the war.

NOTES

THE CANAVANS

THIS play is founded more directly upon folklore and less upon written history than the others, so far as the tradition of the Virgin Queen goes in Ireland. But the epithets given her by her courtiers are taken from the writings of the time. The desire possessing Peter Canavan to be on the safe side, on the side of the strongest, is not bounded by any century or kept within the borders of any country, though it jumps to light more aggressively in one which, like Ireland, has been tilted between two loyalties through so many generations. The play seems (to me now) somewhat remote, inexplicable, as if written less by logical plan than in one of those moments of light-heartedness that comes, as I think, as an inheritance from my French great-grandmother, Frances Aigoin; a moment of that "sudden Glory, the Passion which maketh those Grimaces called Laughter." It plays merrily, and there are some who like it best of my comedies.

As to traditions of the Tudors, this is what I am told in Kiltartan:

"Henry the Eighth was crying and roaring and leaping out of the bed for three days and nights before his death.   And he died cursing his children, and he that had eight millions when he came to the throne, coining leather money at the end.

"Queen Elizabeth was awful.   Beyond everything she was.   When she came to the turn she dyed her hair red, and whatever man she had to do with, she sent him to the block in the morning, that he would be able to tell nothing.   She had an awful temper. She would throw a knife from the table at the waiting ladies, and if anything vexed her she would maybe work upon the floor.   A thousand dresses she left after her.   Very superstitious she was.   Sure after her death they found a card, the ace of hearts, nailed to her chair under the seat.   She thought she would never die while she had it there.   And she bought a bracelet from an old woman out in Wales that was over a hundred years.   It was superstition made her do that, and they found it after her death, tied about her neck.

"It was a town called Calais brought her to her death, and she lay chained on the floor three days and three nights.   The Archbishop was trying to urge her to eat, but she said: 'You would not ask me to do it if you knew the way I am,' for nobody could see the chains.   After her death they waked her for six days in Whitehall, and there were six ladies sitting beside the body every night.   Three coffins were about it, the one nearest the body of lead, and then a wooden one, and a leaden one on the outside. And every night there came from them a great bellow.   And the last night there came a bellow that broke the three coffins open, and tore the velvet,

and there came out a stench that killed the most
of the ladies and a million of the people of London
with the plague. Queen Victoria was more hon-
ourable than that. It would be hard to beat Queen
Elizabeth."

THE WHITE COCKADE

Some time ago I was looking through some poems
taken down in Irish from the country people, and a
line in one of them seemed strange to me "Prebaim
mo chroidhe le mo Stuart glegeal"—"My heart leaps
up with my bright Stuart"; for I had not heard any
songs of this sort in Galway and I remembered that
our Connacht Raftery, whose poems are still teaching
history, dealt very shortly with the Royal Stuarts.
"James," he says, "he was the worst man for habits,
he laid chains on our bogs and mountains. The
father was n't worse than the son Charles, that left
sharp scourges on Ireland. When God and the people
thought it time the story to be done, he lost his head.
The next James—sharp blame to him—gave his
daughter to William as woman and wife; made the
Irish English and the English Irish, like wheat and
oats in the month of harvest. And it was at Aughrim
on a Monday many a son of Ireland found sorrow
without speaking of all that died."
So I went to ask some of the wise old neighbours
who sit in wide chimney nooks by turf fires, and
to whom I go to look for knowledge of many things,
if they knew of any songs in praise of the Stuarts.

But they were scornful. "No indeed," one said,
"there are no songs about them and no praises in the
West, whatever there may be in the South. Why
would there, and they running away and leaving the
country the way they did? And what good did
they ever do it? James the Second was a coward. Why did n't he go into the thick of the
battle like the Prince of Orange? He stopped on a
hill three miles away, and rode off to Dublin, bringing
the best of his troops with him. There was a lady
walking in the street at Dublin when he got there,
and he told her the battle was lost, and she said:
'Faith you made good haste; you made no delay on
the road.' So he said no more after that. The
people liked James well enough before he ran; they
did n't like him after that."

And another said: "Seumas Salach, Dirty James,
it is he brought all down. At the time of the battle
there was one of his men said, 'I have my eye cocked,
and all the nations will be done away with,' and
he pointing his cannon. 'Oh!' said James, 'Don't
make a widow of my daughter.' If he did n't say
that, the English would have been beat. It was a
very poor thing for him to do."

And one who lives on the border of Munster said:
"I used to hear them singing 'The White Cockade'
through the country; King James was beaten and
all his well-wishers; my grief, my boy that went with
them! But I don't think the people had ever much
opinion of the Stuarts, but in those days they were
all prone to versify." And another old man said:

"When I was a young chap knocking about in Connemara, I often heard songs about the Stuarts, and talk of them and of the blackbird coming over the water. But they found it hard to get over James making off after the battle of the Boyne." And when I looked through the lately gathered bundle of songs again, and through some old collections of favourite songs in Irish, I found they almost all belonged to Munster. And if they are still sung there, it is not, as I think, for the sake of the Kings, but for the sake of the poets who wrote them. And in these songs of sorrow for Ireland and the indictment of England, the Stuart himself is often forgotten, or when he appears, he is but a faint and unreal image; a saint by whose name a heavy oath is sworn.

It is different with Patrick Sarsfield, Earl of Lucan, a "great general that killed thousands of the English"; the brave, handsome, fighting man, the descendant of Conall Cearnach, the man who, after the Boyne, offered to "change Kings and fight the battle again." The songs about him are personal enough. Here is one I have put into English:

"O Patrick Sarsfield, health be to you, since you went to France and your camps were loosened; making your sighs along with the King, and you left poor Ireland and the Gael defeated—Och Ochone!

"O Patrick Sarsfield, it is a man with God you are, and blessed is the earth you ever walked on. The blessing of the bright sun and the moon upon you since you took the day from the hands of King William —Och Ochone!

"O Patrick Sarsfield, the prayer of every person with you; my own prayer and the prayer of the Son of Mary with you, since you took the narrow ford going through Biorra, and since in Cuilenn O'Cuanac you won Limerick—Och Ochone!

"They put the first breaking on us at the Bridge of the Boyne; the second breaking at the Bridge of Slaney; the third breaking in Aughrim of O'Kelly; and O sweet Ireland, my five hundred healths to you —Och Ochone!

"O'Kelly has manuring for his land, that is not sand or dung, but ready soldiers doing bravery with pikes, that were left in Aughrim stretched in ridges—Och, Ochone!

"Who is that beyond on the hill Beinn Edar? I, a poor soldier with King James. I was last year in arms and in dress, but this year I am asking alms—Och, Ochone!"

As to the poor Lady, she was not the only one to wander miserably, having spent all for the Stuarts.

The attempted escape of King James in the barrel had already been used by Dr. Hyde in a little play written in Irish. In these days, when so much of the printed history we were taught as children is being cast out by scholars, we must refill the vessel by calling in tradition, or if need be our own imaginings. When my *White Cockade* was first produced I was pleased to hear that J. M. Synge had said my method had made the writing of historical drama again possible.

THE DELIVERER

I used to say in defence of friends of mine, who were attacked for wild acts, and Mr. Yeats borrowed my saying, that Moses was of no use to his people until he had killed an Egyptian. Then I began to say in relation to a "gran rifiuto" of later days that some who had turned upon their leader would have their forty years of walking the sand. More lately in Kiltartan, I was told by one who had been present at the last meeting held by that deserted leader, how those who had crowded to him before had left him by order, and how fiery his words were and how white was his face. And, it was said "The ancient Jews turned against Moses in the same way."

I was at a Feis, a Festival, at Spiddal on Galway Bay in honour of the Irish language about ten years ago, and after it I wrote:

"In the evening there were people waiting round the door to hear the songs and the pipes again. An old man among them was speaking with many gestures, his voice rising, and a crowd gathering about him. 'Tha se beo, tha se beo'—'he is living, he is living,' I heard him say over and over again. I asked what he was saying and was told: 'He says that Parnell is alive yet.' I was pushed away from him by the crowd to where a policeman was looking on. 'He says that Parnell is alive still,' I said. 'There are many say that,' he answered. 'And after all no one ever saw the body that was buried.'"

I remember a visit of M. Paul Bourget to Coole

and his being so excited and moved by the tragic wasted face of one of the last photographs of Mr. Parnell, that he could not leave it but carried it about the house.   I had already written on the back of that portrait this verse from an old ballad:

> Oh, I have dreamed a dreary dream
> Beyond the isle of Skye,
> I saw a dead man win a fight
> And I think that man was I!

Dates and casts of the first production of these plays at the Abbey Theatre, Dublin.

THE CANAVANS was produced December 8, 1906, with the following cast:

Peter Canavan	.	.	.	. W. G. FAY
Antony	.	.	.	J. A. O'ROURKE
Widow Greely	.	.	.	MAIRE O'NEILL
Widow Deeny	.	.	.	BRIGIT O'DEMPSEY
Captain Headley	.	.	.	ARTHUR SINCLAIR

THE WHITE COCKADE was produced December 9, 1905, with the following cast:

Matt Kelleher	.	.	.	. W. G. FAY
Owen Kelleher	.	.	.	. F. WALKER
King James	.	.	.	ARTHUR SINCLAIR
Sarsfield	.	.	.	. F. J. FAY
Carter .	.	.	.	. J. DUNNE
Mrs. Kelleher	.	.	.	. SARA ALLGOOD
Old Lady	.	.	.	. MAIRE NI SHIUBLAIGH
Williamite Soldier		.	.	AMBROSE POWER
Another	.	.	.	. U. WRIGHT
Another	.	.	.	. J. MAGEE
French Sailor	.	.	.	
Another	.	.	.	

197

THE DELIVERER was produced January 12, 1911, with the following cast:

Ard	FRED O'DONOVAN
Malachi	J. A. O'ROURKE
Dan	ARTHUR SINCLAIR
King's Nurseling . . .	J. M. KERRIGAN
Steward	SYDNEY J. MORGAN
Officer	B. MACNAMARA
Ard's Wife . . .	MAIRE NI SHIUBLAIGH
Malachi's Wife . . .	SARA ALLGOOD
Dan's Wife	MAIRE O'NEILL

5